55 classic recipes:
bread
from around the world

55 classic recipes:
bread
from around the world

CHRISTINE INGRAM AND JENNIE SHAPTER

AN IRRESISTIBLE COLLECTION OF TRADITIONAL AND CONTEMPORARY
RECIPES SHOWN IN OVER 280 MOUTHWATERING PHOTOGRAPHS

HERMES
HOUSE

This edition is published by Hermes House,
an imprint of Anness Publishing Limited, Hermes House,
88–89 Blackfriars Road, London SE1 8HA;
tel. 020 7401 2077; fax 020 7633 9499

www.hermeshouse.com; www.annesspublishing.com

If you like the images in this book and would like to
investigate using them for publishing, promotions
or advertising, please visit our website
www.practicalpictures.com for more information.

PUBLISHER Joanna Lorenz
MANAGING EDITOR: Judith Simons
EDITOR: Elizabeth Woodland
DESIGNER: Nigel Partridge
PHOTOGRAPHER: Nicki Dowey
HOME ECONOMIST: Jennie Shapter
PRODUCTION CONTROLLER: Helen Wang

ETHICAL TRADING POLICY
Because of our ongoing ecological investment programme,
you, as our customer, can have the pleasure and reassurance
of knowing that a tree is being cultivated on your behalf to
naturally replace the materials used to make the book
you are holding. For further information about this
scheme, go to www.annesspublishing.com/trees

© Anness Publishing Limited 2008, 2010

Previously published as part of a larger volume,
The World Encyclopedia of Bread and Bread Making

PUBLISHER'S NOTE
Although the advice and information in this book are
believed to be accurate and true at the time of going to
press, neither the authors nor the publisher can accept
any legal responsibility or liability for any errors or
omissions that may be made nor for any inaccuracies nor
for any harm or injury that comes about from following
instructions or advice in this book.

NOTES
Bracketed terms are intended for American readers.
The bread machine recipes in this book have all been
tested and written for use in a variety of machines available from leading manufacturers. For best results, always
refer to your manufacturer's handbook and instructions if
you are unsure, and to confirm the
proportion of flour to liquids.
You may need to adjust the recipes to
suit your machine.
For all recipes, quantities are given in both metric and
imperial measures and, where appropriate, measures are
also given in standard cups and spoons. Follow one set,
but not a mixture, because they are not interchangeable.
Standard spoon and cup measures are level.
1 tsp = 5ml, 1 tbsp = 15ml, 1 cup = 250ml/8fl oz
Australian standard tablespoons are 20ml. Australian
readers should use 3 tsp in place of 1 tbsp for measuring
small quantities of flour, salt, etc.
Medium (US large) eggs are used unless
otherwise stated.

Main cover image shows Shaped Dinner Rolls –
for recipe see page 42

CONTENTS

INTRODUCTION

There is something undeniably special about bread. The flavour of a good loaf, the texture of the soft crumb contrasting with the crispness of the crust, is almost a sensual experience. Who can walk home with a fresh baguette without slowly, almost absent-mindedly breaking off pieces to eat en route? Or resist the promise of a slice of a soft white farmhouse loaf, spread simply with butter? Most people have their own favourite: ciabatta, rich with olive oil; dark, malty rye; honeyed *challah* or a Middle Eastern bread, freshly baked and redolent of herbs and spices. Whatever the shape or texture, bread has a special place in our affections.

Even today, at the start of the 21st century, when bread is taken largely for granted, seen as an accompaniment or a "carrier" for other foods, we still have a sense of its supreme significance. In some languages the word "bread" means "food", and in certain of the more rural parts of Spain and Italy, for example, you may find that bread is blessed or kissed before being broken or eaten. There are numerous rituals and traditions attached to bread. Slashing the dough with a cross or making a sign of the Cross over the loaf before baking was believed to let the devil out. Cutting the bread at both ends was also recommended to rid the house of the devil. One extraordinary custom was

BELOW: Cutting a cross in an unbaked loaf was believed to let the devil out.

ABOVE: Just a few of the many shapes and types of bread.

sin-eating, a practice at funerals, whereby someone would eat a loaf of bread and by so doing would take on the sins of the dead person.

The obvious explanation for bread's importance is that until quite recently, it was for many, quite literally the "staff of life" – the single essential food. Today, most people have more varied diets. Potatoes, pasta and rice are all enjoyed and are important staple foods, but in some countries bread is still the most popular of the carbohydrates, eaten with every meal and in many cases with every course.

Like wine tasters, true aficionados taste bread *au naturel* in order to savour its unique taste and texture, unadulterated by other flavours. Good as this can be, the best thing about bread is that it goes so well with other foods. Throughout Europe bread is most frequently cut or broken into pieces to be eaten with a meal – to mop up soups and sauces or to eat with hams, pâtés and cheese. Dark rye breads, spread with strongly flavoured cheese or topped with smoked fish, are popular in northern Europe, and in the Middle East breads are split and stuffed with meats and salads – a tradition that has been warmly embraced in the West too. In

Britain and the USA, the European custom of serving bread with a meal, with or instead of potatoes or rice, is catching on, but sandwiches are probably still the favourite way of enjoying bread.

Sandwiches have been going strong for a couple of hundred years – invented, it is said, by John Montagu, 4th Earl of Sandwich, so that he could eat a meal without having to leave the gaming table. Although baguettes and bagels are naturally ideally suited for linking bread with meat, the sandwich is unique and continues to be the perfect vehicle for fillings that become more and more adventurous.

Figures show that throughout Europe bread consumption declined after World War II. Until then it was the single most important food in the diet, but due to increased prosperity, which meant a wider choice of other foods, and mass production, which led to bread becoming increasingly insipid and tasteless, people moved away from their "daily bread". The situation was more noticeable in some countries than others. In France, Italy and Spain, where people continued to demand the best, eating of bread did not decline so sharply, although even in those countries, the quality did deteriorate for a time. In Britain, however, most bread was notoriously bland – the ubiquitous white

BELOW: In northern Europe, dark rye bread is served sliced with colourful, rich-tasting toppings.

sliced loaf being little more than a convenient shape for the toaster. In supermarkets, certainly, there was a time, not so long ago, when apart from the standard pre-wrapped white loaf, the only baked goods on sale were croissants and a selection of fruited teabreads, vaguely labelled as "Continental". Yet during the last decade, things have improved by leaps and bounds. Perhaps supermarkets, finding that the smell of freshly baked bread enticed shoppers into their stores, installed more in-store bakeries. Or perhaps shoppers who travelled abroad and sampled the breads of other countries created a demand for better breads made with better flours, using more imaginative recipes and untreated with additives.

Nowadays there is a huge choice of breads both from independent bakeries and from the large supermarkets. Italian ciabatta and focaccia are now a regular sight, even in the smallest food stores, as are the various Spanish, Indian and Middle Eastern breads. There is an increasingly interesting choice of German, Danish, Scandinavian and eastern European breads and, among the French breads, there is now a truly good range on offer. If the supermarket has an in-store bakery, baguettes are likely to be freshly baked and some are now as good as the real thing. The availability of *pains de campagne*, *levains* and other rustic breads means that you can choose breads to suit the style of meal you are serving, while sweet breads, such as brioches and croissants from France, *pane al cioccolato* from Italy and numerous offerings from Germany mean that there is much more to choose from than simply toast at breakfast and malt loaf at tea time.

Local bakers, although competing with the supermarkets, have paradoxically benefited from the range on offer from supermarkets. The more breads there are available, the more people feel inclined to try other baked goods. Small bakers, who could easily have lost customers to the big stores, have risen to the challenge by producing their own range of country-style and fine breads. Craft bakers are producing a variety of breads, at the same time experimenting with recipes they

ABOVE: A huge range of traditionally baked French breads are offered for sale in this specialist bakery.

have devised themselves. Bread making has never been a skill that has stood still. The best craft bakers have ensured that bread making has continued to evolve, resulting in the emergence of all sorts of corn and barley breads, mixed grain loaves and a range of new sourdoughs.

Added to this are the many European-style bakeries. Set up and run by émigrés from all parts of Europe and beyond, these bakeries are the best source of many of the most authentic European breads. In supermarkets you will invariably find ciabatta or focaccia, but for *paesano*, *pagnotta* or *pane sciocco* you

BELOW: Classic country-style breads are enjoying a renaissance.

are likely to need an Italian baker, who will be only too happy to provide you with the loaves and tell you all about them while they are being wrapped.

With so many types of breads available it can be hard to just choose just one. Crusty breads, such as baguettes, round cobs or Italian country loaves, are evenly crusty, although the type of dough, the humidity during proving, the steam in the oven and the heat itself determines whether the crust is fragile or chewy. Loaves, such as the English farmhouse, baked in metal tins, characteristically have a golden top, but with thinner crusts on the sides. Rolls or breads baked up against each other have even softer sides and are described as "batch-baked". Sourdough breads are made without yeast – using a natural leaven instead – and are often labelled as "yeast-free" breads or "naturally leavened". There are many varieties, some made entirely from wheat, some from rye, others from a blend of both of these or other cereals. They are normally heavier than an average loaf, with a dense texture and pleasantly tart flavour.

This wide-ranging kitchen book offers a superb selection of the best breads from around the globe, so you can try as many different types as you wish. All the breads are very simple to make and the instructions are easy-to-follow, and every recipe is illustrated with a picture of the finished bread so you know exactly what you're aiming to achieve.

INGREDIENTS FOR BREAD MAKING

WHEAT FLOURS

The simplest breads are a mixture of flour and water and some type of leavening agent. Beyond that narrow definition, however, lies an infinite number of possibilities. The flour is most likely to come from wheat, but may be derived from another type of grain or even, in the case of buckwheat, from another source entirely. The liquid may be water, but could just as easily be milk, or a mixture. Yeast is the obvious raising agent, but there are other options. Salt is normally essential, fats are often added, and other ingredients range from sweeteners like sugar or molasses to dried fruit, spices and savoury flavourings.

WHITE FLOUR

This flour contains about 75 per cent of the wheat grain with most of the bran and the wheat germ extracted. Plain flour is used for pastry, sauces and biscuits (cookies); while self-raising (self-rising) flour, which contains a raising agent, is used for cakes, scones (US biscuits) and puddings. It can also be used for soda bread. American all-purpose flour is a medium-strength flour, somewhere between the British plain and strong white flour. Soft flour, sometimes known as American cake flour, has been milled very finely for sponge cake and similar bakes.

UNBLEACHED WHITE FLOUR

Unbleached flour is more creamy in colour than other white flours, which have been whitened artificially. Bleaching, which involves treating the flour with chlorine, is becoming increasingly rare and the majority of white flours are unbleached, although check the packet to be sure. In Britain, flour producers are required by law to add, or fortify their white flours with, certain nutrients such as vitamin B1, nictinic acid, iron and calcium. These are often added in the form of white soya flour, which has a natural bleaching effect.

RIGHT: Organic flours are being used increasingly for bread making.

STRONG WHITE/WHITE BREAD FLOUR

For almost all bread making, the best type of flour to use is one which is largely derived from wheat that is high in protein. This type of flour is described as "strong" and is often labelled "bread flour", which underlines its suitability for the task. Proteins in the flour, when mixed with water, combine to make gluten and it is this that gives dough its elasticity when kneaded, and allows it to trap the bubbles of carbon dioxide given off by the yeast. A soft flour produces flat loaves that stale quickly; conversely, if the flour is too hard, the bread will have a coarse texture. A balance is required and most millers blend hard and soft wheats to make a flour that produces a well-flavoured loaf with good volume. Most strong white flours have a lower protein content than their wholemeal equivalent and a baker would probably use a flour with a protein level of 12 per cent. The protein value of a flour can be found listed on the side of the packet under "Nutritional Value".

FINE FRENCH PLAIN FLOUR

French bakers use a mixture of white bread flour and fine plain flour to make baguettes and other specialities. Fine French plain flour is called *farine fluide* in its country of origin because it is so light and free-flowing. Such is the popularity of French-style baked goods that this type of flour is now available in supermarkets.

WHOLEMEAL (WHOLE-WHEAT) FLOUR

This flour is made using the whole of the wheat grain and is sometimes called 100 per cent extraction flour: nothing is added and nothing is taken away. The bran and wheat germ, which are automatically separated from the white inner portion if milled between rollers, are returned to the white flour at the end of the process. *Atta* is a fine wholemeal flour used for Indian breads (see Other Flours).

STONEGROUND WHOLEMEAL FLOUR

This wholemeal flour has been ground in the traditional way between two stones. The bran and wheat germ are milled with the rest of the wheat grain, so there is no separation of the flour at any stage. Stoneground flour is also considered to have a better flavour, owing to the slow grinding of the stones. However, because the oily wheat germ is squashed into the flour, rather than churned in later, stoneground flour has a higher fat content and may become rancid if stored for too long.

ORGANIC WHOLEMEAL FLOUR

This flour has been milled from organic wheat, which is wheat produced without the use of artificial fertilizers or pesticides. There are organic versions of all varieties of wholemeal and white flours available from most large supermarkets and health-food stores.

STRONG WHOLEMEAL/ WHOLEMEAL BREAD FLOUR

A higher proportion of high gluten wheat is necessary in wholemeal flours to counteract the heaviness of the bran. If the flour is not strong enough, the dough may rise unevenly and is likely to collapse in the oven. The miller selects his grist (the blend) of hard and soft wheat grains, according to the type of flour required. Bakers would probably look for a protein content of about 13.5 per cent; the strong flours available in supermarkets are normally between 11.5 and 13 per cent.

ABOVE: Clockwise from top right: strong white flour, stoneground wholemeal, wholemeal, wheat germ, organic wholemeal, plain white flour, organic plain flour, semolina, organic stoneground wholemeal and Granary flour. The three flours in the centre are (clockwise from top) brown, spelt and self-raising flour.

GRANARY FLOUR

Granary (whole-wheat) is the proprietary name of a blend of brown and rye flours and malted wheat grain. The malted grain gives this bread its characteristic sweet and slightly sticky flavour and texture. It is available from health food stores and supermarkets.

MALTHOUSE FLOUR

A speciality flour available from some large supermarkets and health food stores, this is a combination of stoneground brown flour, rye flour and malted wheat flour with malted wheat flakes. It resembles Granary flour.

GRAHAM FLOUR

This popular American flour is slightly coarser than ordinary wholemeal. It is named after a 19th-century Connecticut cleric, Rev. Sylvestor Graham, who developed the flour and advocated using the whole grain for bread making because of the beneficial effects of the bran.

BROWN FLOUR

This flour contains about 85 per cent of the original grain, with some of the bran and wheat germ extracted. It produces a lighter loaf than 100 per cent wholemeal flour, while still retaining a high percentage of wheat germ, which gives bread so much of its flavour.

WHEAT GERM FLOUR

A wheat germ flour can be brown or white but must contain at least 10 per cent added wheat germ. Wheat germ is highly nutritious and this bread is considered particularly healthy. Wheat germ bread has a pleasant nutty flavour.

SEMOLINA

This is the wheat kernel or endosperm, once the bran and wheat germ have been removed from the grain by milling, but before it is fully milled into flour. Semolina can be ground either coarsely or finely and is used for certain Indian breads, including *bhatura*.

SPELT

Although spelt, a variety of wheat, is no longer widely grown, one or two smaller flour mills still produce a spelt flour, which is available in some health food stores.

OTHER FLOURS

Alternative grains, such as barley, corn-meal and oatmeal, are full of flavour but contain little or no gluten. Breads made solely from them would rise poorly and would be extremely dense. The milled grains are therefore often mixed with strong wheat flour. Rye is rich in gluten, but pure rye doughs are difficult to handle; once again the addition of strong wheat flour can provide a solution.

BARLEY MEAL

Barley is low in gluten and is seldom used for bread making in Britain and western Europe. In Russia and other eastern European countries, however, barley loaves continue to be produced, the flour mostly blended with some proportion of wheat or rye flour to give the loaf volume. These loaves are definitely on the robust side. They tend to be rather grey and flat and have an earthy, rather mealy flavour. Similar loaves must have been baked in parts of the British Isles in the past, when times were hard or the wheat harvest had failed. There are several old Welsh recipes for barley bread, which was rolled out flat before being baked on a baking stone.

Barley meal is the ground whole grain of the barley, while barley flour is ground pearl barley, with the outer skin removed.

BELOW: Traditional Anadama bread is made from a combination of corn meal, white flour and wholemeal flour.

Either can be added in small quantities to wholemeal or to white flour to produce a bread with a slightly rustic flavour.

BUCKWHEAT FLOUR

This grain is blackish in colour, hence its French name, *blé noir*. It is not strictly a cereal but is the fruit of a plant belonging to the dock family. The three-cornered grains are milled to a flour and used for pancakes, blinis and, in France, for crêpes or galettes. It can also be added to wheat flour and is popular mixed with other grains in multigrained loaves. It has a distinctive, earthy flavour and is best used in small quantities.

CORNMEAL (MAIZEMEAL)

This meal is ground from white or yellow corn and is normally available in coarse, medium or fine grinds. Coarse-ground corn meal is used for the Italian dish of polenta; for bread making choose one of the finer grinds, available from most health food stores. There are numerous corn breads from the southern states of America, including the famous double corn bread. Corn was brought back to Europe by the Spanish and Portuguese and corn breads are still popular in these countries today, particularly in Portugal. Corn contains no gluten so will not make a loaf unless it is blended with wheat flour, in which case the corn adds a pleasant flavour and colour.

MILLET FLOUR

Although high in protein, millet flour is low in gluten and is not commonly used by itself in bread making. It is pale yellow in colour, with a gritty texture. The addition of wheat flour produces an interesting, slightly nutty flavour.

OATMEAL

Oatmeal does not contain gluten and is only very rarely used by itself for bread making. The exception is in Scotland where flat crisply baked oatmeal biscuits have been popular for centuries. These are baked on a griddle and served with butter or marmalade. Oatmeal can also be used in wheat or multigrained loaves. Choose finely ground oatmeal for making oatcakes or for using in loaves. Rolled oats are not a flour but are the steamed and flattened whole oats. They look good scattered over the crust of leaves and rolls, and add a pleasant flavour.

RICE FLOUR

Polished rice, if ground very finely, becomes rice flour. It can be used as a thickening agent and is useful for people with wheat allergies. It is also occasionally used for some Indian breads.

STORAGE

Although most flours keep well, they do not last indefinitely and it is important to pay attention to the "use-by" date on the packet. Old flour will begin to taste stale and will make a disappointing loaf. Always store flour on a cool dry shelf. Ideally, the flour should be kept in its bag and placed in a tin or storage jar with a tight-fitting lid. Wash and dry the jar thoroughly whenever replacing with new flour and avoid adding new flour to old. Wholemeal (whole-wheat) flour, because it contains the oils in wheatgerm, keeps less well than white flours. Consequently, do not buy large quantities at a time and keep it in a very cool place or in the salad drawer of the refrigerator.

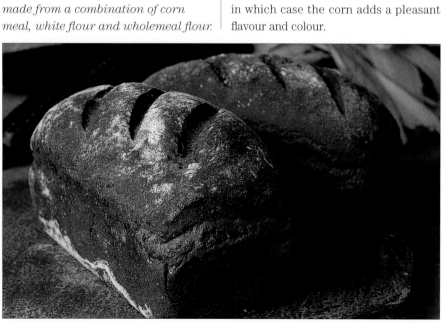

ABOVE: A selection of non-wheat grains and specialist flours. Clockwise from top centre: rye flour, buckwheat flour, corn meal, bajra flour, organic rye flour, millet grain, jowar flour, gram flour and atta or chapati flour. In the centre are (clockwise from top) barley meal, fine oatmeal and rice flour.

RYE FLOUR

Rye is the only other cereal, apart from wheat, that is widely used to make bread. It has a good gluten content, although the gluten in rye is different from wheat gluten, and rye doughs are notoriously sticky and difficult to handle. For this reason, rye meal is often blended with other flours to create a dough that is more manageable. There are as many different rye meals as there are wheat flours, ranging in colour and in type of grind. Pumpernickel and other dense and steamed box-shaped rye breads use a coarsely ground wholemeal rye, while finer flour, which contains neither the bran nor the germ, is used for the popular crusty black breads.

INDIAN FLOURS

ATTA/CHAPATI FLOUR

This is a very fine wholemeal (whole-wheat) flour, which is normally found only in Indian grocers where it is sometimes labelled *ata*. As well as being used to make chapatis, it is also the type of flour used for making rotis and other Indian flat breads.

BAJRA FLOUR

This plant grows along the west coast of India. The grains are a mixture of yellow and grey but when ground, the flour is a more uniform grey. It has a strong nutty aroma and a distinct flavour. *Bajra* bread or *rotla* is cooked, like all unleavened breads, on a griddle.

JOWAR FLOUR

Jowar grows over most of central and southern India. The flour, ground from the pretty pale yellow grains, is a creamy-white colour. The flat breads usually made from this flour, called *bhakris*, are roasted on a griddle and are traditionally served with a rich-flavoured, spicy, coconut, garlic and red chilli chutney.

GRAM FLOUR

This is a flour made from ground chickpeas. It is also known as *besan*. The Indian missi rotis – spicy, unleavened breads from northern India – are made using gram flour or a mixture of whole-wheat and gram flours.

YEAST AND OTHER LEAVENS

Almost all breads today are leavened in some way, which means that a substance has been added to the dough to initiate fermentation and make the dough rise.

Without yeast or another leavening agent, the mixture of flour and water, once cooked, would be merely a flat, unappetizing cake. At some point in our history, our ancestors discovered how dough, if left to ferment in the warmth, produced a lighter and airier bread when cooked.

The transformation of dough into bread is caused by yeast or another leavening ingredient producing carbon dioxide. The carbon dioxide expands, the dough stretches and tiny pockets of air are introduced into the dough. When the bread is cooked the process is set and the air becomes locked in.

LEAVENING AGENTS

The most popular and most widely known leavening ingredient in bread making is yeast. However, raising agents such as

BELOW: Clockwise from top left: fresh yeast, dried yeast, fast-action dried yeast and easy-blend dried yeast.

bicarbonate of soda (baking soda) and baking powder are also used for making certain breads.

YEAST

Yeast is the most popular leavening agent for bread making. It is simple to use, more reliable than a natural leaven and considerably quicker to activate. Conventional dried yeast, easy-blend (rapid-rise) and fast-action yeast are all types of dried yeast, produced for the convenience of those making bread at home. Almost all bakers prefer fresh yeast, since it is considered to have a superior flavour and to be more reliable. However, when fresh yeast is not available or convenient, dried yeast is a handy substitute.

There are several ways of adding yeast to flour. Fresh yeast is usually blended with lukewarm water before being mixed into the flour; conventional dried yeast is first reconstituted in warm water and then left until frothy; easy-blend and fast-action dried yeasts are added directly to the flour.

THE SPONGE METHOD

Some yeasted breads are made by the sponge method, whereby the yeast is dissolved in more lukewarm water than usual, and then mixed with some of the flour to make a batter. This can be done in a bowl, or the batter can be made in a well in the centre of the flour, with only some surrounding flour included at the start, as in the recipe for split tin loaf. The batter is left for at least 20 minutes – often much longer – until bubbles appear on the surface, a process known as sponging. It is then mixed with the remaining flour, and any other ingredients are added. The advantage of this method is that it enables the yeast to start working without being inhibited by ingredients like eggs, fat and sugar, which slow down its action.

Many French breads are also sponged. A slightly different technique is used and the batter is left to ferment for a lot longer – for 2–12 hours. The slow fermentation creates what is described as a *poolish* sponge, and makes for a wonderfully flavoured bread, with very little acidity, yet with a fragile and crunchy crust. *Pain polka* is made by this method, as are the best baguettes. Two factors affect the rise: the temperature of the room and the wetness of the mixture. A wet sponge will rise more quickly than a firmer one. Italian bakers employ a similar process called a *biga*. This uses less liquid and the sponge takes about 12–15 hours to mature. For an example of the use of a *biga* starter, see the recipe for ciabatta.

BAKING POWDER

This is made up of a mixture of acid and alkaline chemicals. When these come into contact with moisture, as in a dough or a batter, the reaction of the chemicals produces tiny bubbles of air so the dough rises and becomes spongy, just as it does with yeast. Unlike when making yeast-leavened breads, however, it is important to work fast as the carbon dioxide will quickly escape and the loaf will collapse.

BICARBONATE OF SODA

Bicarbonate of soda (baking soda), sometimes just called soda, is the leavening ingredient in Irish soda bread. It is an alkaline chemical which, when mixed with an acid in a moisture-rich environment, reacts to produce carbon dioxide. Cream of tartar, an acid that is made from fermented grapes, is commonly used in conjunction with bicarbonate of soda for soda breads, or else the soda is combined with soured milk, which is naturally acidic. Buttermilk may also be used.

LEFT: Pain de campagne is one of the many French sourdough breads.

BREWER'S YEAST

Old cookbooks sometimes call for brewer's yeast or ale or beer barm. Until the last century, this was the common and only leavening ingredient. Since then brewer's yeast has acquired something of a cult status, and during the 1950s in the USA and Britain it was considered a wonder food owing to its nutritional value. It is not however, suitable for bread making, being too bitter, and should only be used for making beer.

NATURAL LEAVENS

Natural leavens, made using a medium of flour, or grown from potatoes, yogurt, treacle or buttermilk, were once very popular and are enjoying a renaissance.

SOURDOUGHS

Sourdoughs are breads based on a natural leaven. An authentic sourdough relies entirely on the wild yeasts that exist in the air. Given the right conditions, any dough of flour and water or batter of vegetable origin will start to ferment spontaneously and will continue to do so if starch or sugar is added to feed it. Recipes for some of the traditional American and German breads use a variety of rather surprising starters for their sourdoughs, from potatoes to treacle. With the renewed interest in rustic breads, there are all sorts of sourdough breads in supermarkets and specialist bakers, and numerous books explaining how to make them at home.

There are many, many types of sourdough. In France the sourdough method is known as the *chef* or *levain*, and is used for *pain de campagne* as well as for sourdough baguettes.

Despite their many variations, sourdoughs do have some elements in common. Each begins with a "starter", which can take anything up to a week to ferment and become established. This "starter" or leaven is used, daily by bakers or less frequently by home bread makers, for the day's bread. A small amount of the dough is then kept back and used for the next batch of bread. Alternatively, a slightly more liquid starter can be made and kept in the refrigerator until it is ready for use. Each time part of the starter is used, the remaining starter is refreshed with equal amounts of flour and water. Looked after in this way, some starters have been known to survive for years.

Starters for sourdoughs, as well as the breads themselves, vary hugely – not only from country to country but from village to village. Many recipes, and indeed many bakers, recommend using a little yeast to get started since a true starter is likely to be rather a hit-or-miss affair. Wild yeasts may be all around us, but for some reason they seem to vanish as soon as you decide to make a sourdough. Starters also improve with age, so do not be discouraged if your first sourdoughs are rather bland. After a few attempts, you should find your breads developing their own tangy personality.

YEAST KNOW-HOW

◆ Yeast needs warmth to activate it, but must not be subjected to too hot a temperature or it will die. Whether dissolving yeast in water or adding liquid to the yeast and flour, make sure the liquid is not too warm. The optimum heat is 38°C/100°F. If you do not have a thermometer, experts recommend mixing 300ml/½ pint/1¼ cups boiling water with 600ml/1pint/2½ cups cold water, and measuring the required water from the mixture.

◆ If you are using easy-blend or fast-action dried yeast you can afford to have the water slightly hotter, since the yeast is mixed with the flour, and the heat of the water will rapidly dissipate.

◆ Check "use-by" dates on dried and fast-action yeasts. If a product is past its "use-by" date, replace it. If it is marginal and you cannot immediately replace it, take a measuring jug (cup) and pour in 120ml/4fl oz/½ cup warm water (43–46°C/110–115°F). Add 5ml/1 tsp sugar, stir to dissolve and then sprinkle over 10ml/2 tsp dried yeast. Stir and leave for 10 minutes. The yeast should begin to rise to the surface after the first 5 minutes, and by 10 minutes there should have developed a rounded crown of foam that reaches to the 250ml/8fl oz/1 cup level of the measuring jug. If this happens the yeast is active; if not, the yeast has lost its potency and should be discarded.

◆ The amount of yeast you require should not increase proportionally as the amount of flour increases, so take care if you decide to double the quantities in a recipe. You will not need to double the amount of yeast. Similarly, if you halve a recipe, you are likely to need proportionally more yeast or be prepared to wait longer for the bread to rise.

ADDITIONAL INGREDIENTS

ABOVE: Welsh bara brith is packed with dried fruits.

Although flour and yeast are the most obvious ingredients used in bread making, there are a number of other ingredients that are just as important.

WATER OR MILK

As a general rule, savoury loaves are made using water; teabreads and sweeter breads use milk. Whatever the liquid, it is always heated slightly. Breads made with milk are softer in both the crumb and the crust than those using water.

SALT

Almost all bread recipes add salt at the beginning, stirring or sifting it right into the flour.

Salt is one of the few essential ingredients in bread making. It is important for both flavour and the effect it has on the yeast and dough. Essentially, it slows down the yeast's action – which is why it should not be added directly to the yeast. This means that the dough rises in a controlled and even way, giving a well-risen even loaf. Too little salt means the loaf will stale more quickly; too much and the crust will harden, so do take care when measuring salt.

LEFT: The French petit pains au lait, made with milk rather than water; have a lovely soft crumb and crust.

SUGAR

Sugar, once invariably added to all breads (usually with the yeast), is now no longer necessary for savoury breads since modern yeasts can be activated without it. However, some bakers still prefer to add a little sugar, even when making savoury baked goods, contending that results with sugar are better than when it is omitted.

White and brown sugar, honey, treacle (molasses) and golden (light corn) syrup can be used to sweeten teabreads and fruit breads. Sugars are normally added with the flour, while syrups are more often stirred into the lukewarm liquid so that they are gently warmed as well.

BUTTER AND EGGS

Enriched breads are made with the addition of both butter and eggs and normally use milk rather than water. These breads, such as panettone, barm brack and many other festive European breads, have a delicious cake-like texture and soft crust. The butter is either melted or diced and the eggs beaten before being worked into other ingredients to make a fairly sticky batter. This is then beaten by hand or in an electric mixer. In some instances, the butter is kneaded into the dough after the initial rising, since large quantities of butter can inhibit the action of the yeast.

BELOW: Panettone is enriched with eggs and egg yolks.

ABOVE: Light fluffy pastry and butter is the key to the perfect croissant.

BELOW: Red lentil dosas are spiced with turmeric and black pepper.

FRUIT

Almost any dried fruit can be added to bread. Raisins, sultanas (golden raisins), currants and mixed (candied) peel have always been popular for fruit loaves. Chopped dates, apricots and prunes can all be kneaded in, as can more exotic fruits, such as dried mango or papaya. Fruit can be added to a dough during mixing or left until the second kneading. If adding at the second kneading, warm the fruit first, so that it does not inhibit the action of the yeast. If you are using an electric mixer or food processor for kneading, note that the blades will chop the fruit. This spoils both the appearance and the flavour of the loaf, so only knead by machine to begin with, then knead the fruit in by hand after the initial rising.

FATS

Fats, in the form of butter, oil, lard (shortening) or vegetable fat, are sometimes added to savoury loaves. They add flavour and help to preserve the freshness of the loaf. The Italians particularly love adding olive oil to their breads, which they do in generous quantities. Although oils and melted butter can be poured into the flour with the yeast and liquid, solid butter or fats are normally kneaded into the flour before the liquid is added.

NUTS, HERBS AND OTHER SAVOURY INGREDIENTS

Some of our favourite breads today are flavoured with herbs, nuts and other

BELOW: Ciabatta, like many Italian breads, is made with olive oil.

such savoury ingredients. *Manoucher*, "Mediterranean nights" bread, is a rainbow of colours. Based on the Italian *focaccia*, it contains rosemary, red, green and yellow (bell) peppers along with goat's cheese. The Italians add olives or sun-dried tomatoes to their ciabatta, while walnut bread (*pain aux noix* in France, *pane con noci* in Italy) is one of the best-known and best-loved savoury loaves.

Nuts, herbs, pitted olives and sun-dried tomatoes should be roughly chopped before being kneaded into the dough after the first rising.

SPICES

The sweet spices are cinnamon, nutmeg, cloves and ginger, and for savoury breads cumin, fennel, caraway and anise impart a delicious flavour. Mace, pepper and coriander seeds can be used for both sweet and savoury breads. Spices can be added with the flour or kneaded in with fruit or nuts, or other ingredients.

BREAD-MAKING TECHNIQUES

USING YEAST

There are several different forms of yeast, some easier to use than others, but none of them particularly tricky if you follow a few simple rules. Whichever yeast you use, it must be in good condition – neither old nor stale – and must not be subjected to too much heat.

USING FRESH YEAST

Fresh yeast is available from baker's stores, health food stores and most supermarkets with an in-store bakery. It is pale beige, has a sweet, fruity smell and should crumble easily. It can be stored in the refrigerator, wrapped in clear film (plastic wrap), for up to 2 weeks or can be frozen for up to 3 months. A quantity of 15g/½oz fresh yeast should be sufficient for 675–900g/ 1½–2lb/6–8 cups flour, although this will depend on the recipe.

1 Put the yeast in a small bowl. Using a spoon, mash or "cream" it with a little of the measured water until smooth.

2 Pour in the remaining measured liquid, which may be water, milk or a mixture of the two. Mix well. Use as directed in the recipe.

USING DRIED YEAST

Dried yeast is simply the dehydrated equivalent of fresh yeast, but it needs to be blended with lukewarm liquid before use. Store dried yeast in a cool dry place and check the "use-by" date on the can or packet. You will need about 15g/½oz (7.5ml/1½ tsp) dried yeast for 675g/ 1½lb/6 cups flour. Some bakers add sugar or honey to the liquid to which the yeast is added, but this is not necessary, as the granules contain enough nourishment to enable the yeast to work.

1 Pour the measured lukewarm liquid into a small bowl and sprinkle the dried yeast evenly over the surface.

2 Cover with clear film and leave in a warm room for 10–15 minutes until frothy. Stir well and use as directed.

WATER TEMPERATURE
For fresh and regular dried yeast, use lukewarm water; for easy-blend and fast-action yeast the water can be a little hotter, as the yeast is mixed with flour before the liquid is added.

USING EASY-BLEND (RAPID-RISE) AND FAST-ACTION DRIED YEASTS

These are the most convenient of the dried yeasts as they can be stirred directly into the flour. Fast-action yeasts and some easy-blends contain a bread improver, which eliminates the need for two kneadings and risings – check the instructions on the packet to make sure. Most of these yeasts come in 7g/¼oz sachets, which are sufficient for 675g/ 1½lb/6 cups flour. Do not store opened sachets as the yeast will deteriorate quickly.

Sift together the flour and salt into a medium bowl and rub in the fat, if using. Stir in the easy-blend or fast-action dried yeast, then add warm water or milk, plus any other ingredients, as directed in the recipe.

BELOW: Small, shaped rolls are very quick to make using easy-blend yeast.

MAKING A YEAST DOUGH BY THE SPONGE METHOD

This method produces bread with an excellent flavour and soft texture. The quantities listed are merely an example and can be increased proportionately. See individual recipes.

1 Mix 7g/¼oz fresh yeast with 250ml/8fl oz/1 cup lukewarm water in a large bowl. Stir in 115g/4oz/1 cup unbleached plain (all-purpose) flour, using a wooden spoon, then use your fingers to draw the mixture together until you have a smooth liquid with the consistency of a thick batter. (Do not add salt to the sponge as this would inhibit the yeast.)

2 Cover with a damp dishtowel and leave in a warm place. The sponge will double or triple in bulk and then fall back, which indicates it is ready to use (after about 5–6 hours).

3 The sponge starter is now ready to be mixed to a dough with the remaining flour and any other ingredients, such as butter as directed in the recipe.

MAKING AN ITALIAN STARTER (*BIGA*)

If you wish to make an Italian *biga* for Pugliese or a similar Italian country bread, use 175g/6oz/1½ cups unbleached plain flour. Cream the yeast with 90ml/6 tbsp lukewarm water, then pour it into a well in the centre of the flour. Gradually mix in the surrounding flour to form a firm dough. The dough should be kneaded for a few minutes and then left, covered with lightly oiled clear film (plastic wrap) for 12–15 hours.

MAKING A FRENCH SOURDOUGH STARTER (*CHEF*)

It is not difficult to make a sourdough starter. The starter can be kept in the refrigerator for up to 10 days, but for longer than that it should be frozen. Bring the starter to room temperature before adding to the next batch of bread.

1 Place 115g/4oz/1 cup flour in a large bowl and add 75ml/5 tbsp water. Mix together, then knead for 3–4 minutes to form a dough. Cover the bowl with clear film and set aside at room temperature for 2–3 days. The flour that you choose will depend on the bread you wish to make; it can be wholemeal (whole-wheat), white or rye, or a combination of two or three.

2 After 2–3 days, the mixture will rise and aerate slightly and turn a greyish colour. A soft crust may form on top of the starter and it should develop a slightly sweet-sour smell.

3 Remove any crust that has formed on top of the starter and discard. Stir in 120ml/4fl oz/½ cup lukewarm water to make a paste and then add 175g/6oz/1½ cups flour. The flour can be wholemeal or a mixture of wholemeal and white. Mix together to make a dough, then transfer to a work surface and knead lightly until firm.

SOURDOUGH

The actual word "sourdough" is thought to have come from America as this style of bread was commonly made by pioneers and the word was sometimes used to describe old "Forty-Niners". However bread made by the sourdough method dates back long before the 19th century. Many traditional European rye breads are based on this method, particularly in Germany and Scandinavia where the sour flavour of the leaven complements the flavour of the rye.

In Britain sourdoughs are sometimes called acids or acid breads. Some restaurants and home bread makers have their own favourite acid breads, but generally there is not much of a tradition of sourdoughs in the British Isles. Except in Ireland, where soda was popular, ale barm (the fermentation liquor from beer) was the most commonly used leaven for bread making until it was replaced by baker's yeast around the middle of the last century.

4 Place the ball of dough in a bowl, cover again with clear film and leave for 1–2 days at room temperature.

5 Remove and discard any crust that forms. What remains – the *chef* – can now be used to make a sourdough bread, such as *pain de campagne rustique*. To keep the *chef* going, save about 225g/8oz of the dough each time.

6 Place the dough starter in a crock or bowl, cover and keep in the refrigerator for up to 10 days or freeze.

MIXING, KNEADING AND RISING

The sequence and method of adding ingredients to make your dough are vital. For some breads, fresh or dried yeast is dissolved in lukewarm water and then stirred into the flour; if easy-blend (rapid-rise) dried yeast or fast-action dried yeast is used, this is added directly to the flour with warm water or milk added afterwards. Read your recipe carefully before starting and warm your bowls if they are in the least bit chilly, so that the yeast gets off to a good start.

MIXING

The easiest way to mix the dough is with your hand but, if you prefer, start mixing with a spoon until the mixture is too stiff to stir, then mix by hand.

1 If using fresh or regular dried yeast, mix it with lukewarm water or milk as described in the recipe. Sift the flour, salt and any other dry ingredients (including easy-blend or fast-action dried yeast, if using) into a large, warm mixing bowl.

2 If using butter or lard (shortening), rub it in. Make a well in the centre of the flour mixture and pour in the yeast mixture with the remaining lukewarm water. If oil is being used, add it now.

3 Mix the liquid into the flour using your hand, stirring in a smooth, wide motion so that all the dry ingredients are evenly incorporated and the mixture forms a dough. Knead lightly in the bowl.

KNEADING

Kneading is something you just cannot skip in bread making. If you do not have strong wrists, or simply do not enjoy it, you will have to resort to using the food processor, which takes all the effort – and much of the time – out of kneading. Better still though, learn to love it.

Kneading dough, whether by hand or machine, is the only way of warming and stretching the gluten in the flour. As the strands of gluten warm and become more elastic, so the dough becomes more springy. It is the elasticity of the dough, combined with the action of the yeast, that gives bread its light, springy texture. Insufficient kneading means that the dough cannot hold the little pockets of air, and the bread will collapse in the oven to leave a heavy and dense loaf.

HOW TO KNEAD BY HAND

1 Place the mixed dough on a floured surface and flour your hands generously.

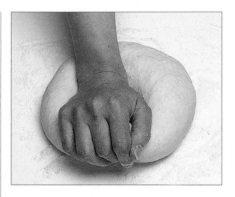

2 Press the heel of your hand firmly into the centre of the dough, then curl your fingers around the edge of the dough.

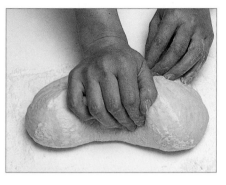

3 Pull and stretch the dough towards you and press down again, giving the dough a quarter turn as you do so.

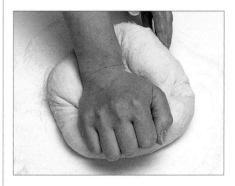

4 Continue pressing and stretching the dough, making quarter turns so that it is evenly kneaded. After about 10 minutes the dough should be supple and elastic; however, some breads need more kneading, so do check the recipe.

ADDING EXTRA INGREDIENTS

Ingredients, such as olives, can be added after kneading, or they can be kneaded in after the first rising.

KNEADING IN A FOOD PROCESSOR

Unless you have an industrial-size machine, it is likely that your food processor will only be able to knead moderate amounts of dough. Don't attempt to knead more dough than recommended by the manufacturer as it may damage the motor. If necessary, knead in small batches and then knead the dough balls together by hand afterwards.

Fit the dough blade into the processor and then blend together all the dry ingredients. Add the yeast mixture, and extra lukewarm liquid and butter or oil, if required; process until the mixture comes together. Knead for 60 seconds, or according to the manufacturer's instructions, then knead by hand on a floured board for 1–2 minutes.

KNEADING IN A FOOD MIXER

Check the manufacturer's instructions to make sure bread dough can be kneaded in your machine.

Mix the dry ingredients together. Add the yeast, liquid and oil or butter, if using, and mix slowly, using the dough hook. The dough will tumble and fall to begin with, and then it will slowly come together. Continue kneading the dough for 3–4 minutes or according to the manufacturer's instructions.

RISING

This is the easy part of bread making – all you need now is to give the dough the right conditions, and nature and chemistry will do the rest. While kneading works and conditions the gluten in the flour, during rising the yeast does the work. The fermentation process creates carbon dioxide, which is trapped within the dough by the elastic gluten. This process also has the effect of conditioning the flour, improving the flavour and texture of the eventual loaf.

The number of times you leave your bread to rise will depend on the yeast you are using and the recipe. An easy-blend or a fast-action yeast needs no first rising, but dough using fresh yeast and other dried yeasts normally requires two risings, with some recipes calling for even more.

TEMPERATURE AND TIME

For most recipes, dough is left to rise at a temperature of about 24–27°C/75–80°F, the equivalent of an airing cupboard or near a warm oven. At a cooler temperature the bread rises more slowly and some of the best-flavoured breads, including baguettes, use a slower rising, giving the enzymes and starches in the flour more time to mature. The quantity of yeast used will also determine the time required for rising. More yeast means quicker rising.

1 Place the kneaded dough in a bowl that has been lightly greased. This will prevent the dough from sticking. Cover the bowl with a damp dishtowel or a piece of oiled clear film (plastic wrap), to prevent a skin from forming on top.

2 Leave to rise until the dough has doubled in bulk. At room temperature, this should take 1½–2 hours – less if the temperature is warmer; more if the room is cool. It can even be left to rise in the refrigerator for about 8 hours.

A FEW SIMPLE RULES

◆ Warm bowls and other equipment.

◆ Use the correct amount of yeast: too much will speed up the rising process but will spoil the flavour and will mean the loaf stales more quickly.

◆ If you have a thermometer, check the temperature of the lukewarm liquid, at least until you can gauge it accurately yourself. It should be between 37–43°C/98–108°F. Mixing two parts cold water with one part boiling water gives you water at roughly the right temperature.

◆ The amount of liquid required for a dough depends on several factors – type of flour, other ingredients, even the room temperature. Recipes therefore often give approximate quantities of liquid. You will soon learn to judge the ideal consistency of a dough.

◆ Do not skimp on kneading. Kneading is essential for stretching the gluten to give a well-risen, light-textured loaf.

◆ Avoid leaving dough to rise in a draught and make sure the ambient temperature is not too high, or the dough will begin to cook.

◆ Always cover the bowl during rising as a crust will form on top of the dough if the air gets to it. Clear film can be pressed on to the dough itself or can be stretched over the bowl. Either way, oil the film first or the dough will stick to it as it rises.

◆ Remember: the slower the rising, the better the taste of the bread.

KNOCKING BACK, SHAPING AND FINAL RISING

KNOCKING BACK

After all the effort by the yeast to create a risen dough, it seems a shame to knock it back. However, this process not only redistributes the gases in the dough that were created by fermentation, it also reinvigorates the yeast, making sure that it is evenly distributed, and ensures the bread has an even texture. It should take only a few minutes and the bread is then ready for shaping. The dough is fully risen when it has doubled in bulk. If you are not sure that it is ready, test by gently inserting a finger into the centre of the dough. The dough should not immediately spring back. If it does, leave for a little longer.

1 Knock back the risen dough using your knuckles. Americans call this "punching down the dough", which is an accurate description of the process. Having knocked back the dough, place it on a floured work surface and knead lightly for 1–2 minutes.

SHAPING

There are several ways of shaping the dough to fit a loaf tin (pan).

1 The easiest way is to shape the dough roughly into an oval and place it in the tin, with the smooth side on top.

2 Alternatively, roll out the dough into a rectangle, a little longer than the tin. Roll it up like a Swiss roll, tuck in the ends and place the roll in the tin, with the seam side down.

3 Another method for shaping the dough is to roll it out into a rectangle and fold it in half lengthways, pinching the edges together on the sides and flattening the dough out slightly with the heel of your hand. Fold the dough over once more to make a double thickness and pinch the edges together again. Now gently roll the dough backwards and forwards until it has a well-rounded shape.

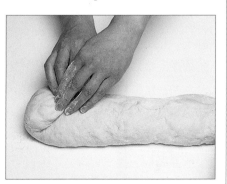

4 Fold in the two short ends and place the dough in the prepared tin with the seam along the bottom.

SHAPING A COB LOAF

1 Shape the dough into a round and then press along the centre with your hand. Turn the dough over, so that the smooth side is uppermost.

2 Shape the dough into a round or oval and place it on a baking sheet.

TIPS

◆ Always knock back the dough after the first rising and knead lightly to redistribute the yeast and the gases formed by fermentation, otherwise you may end up with large holes in the loaf or the crust may lift up and become detached from the crumb.

◆ Rising the dough in a warm place is not always necessary – it is simply a method of speeding up the process. Dough will rise (albeit very slowly) even in the refrigerator. However, wherever you decide to rise your dough the temperature must be constant. Avoid draughts or hot spots, as both will spoil the bread and may cause it to bake unevenly.

◆ Some breads may need slashing either before final rising or during this period (see next section).

Shaping a Baguette

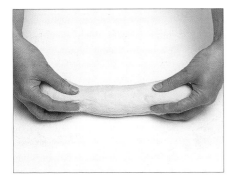

1 Divide the dough into equal pieces. Shape each piece into a ball and then into a rectangle measuring 15 × 7.5cm/ 6 × 3in. Fold the bottom third up and the top third down lengthways. Press the edges together to seal them. Repeat twice, then stretch each piece to a 33–35cm/13–14in loaf.

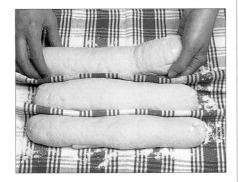

2 Place within the folds of a pleated, floured dishtowel or in *bannetons*.

Shaping a Plait

1 Divide the dough into three equal pieces. Roll each piece into a 25cm/10in sausage about 4cm/1½in thick.

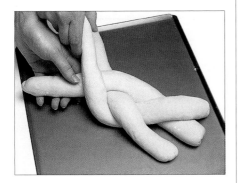

2 Place the three "sausages" on a greased baking sheet. Either start the plait (braid) in the centre, plaiting to each end in turn, or pinch the pieces firmly together at one end then plait.

3 When you have finished, pinch the ends together, and turn them under.

Final Rising

After shaping the dough and placing it on the baking sheet or in the tin (pan), there is usually a final rising before baking. Depending on the warmth of the room, this can take ¾–1½ hours and in a very cool room up to 4 hours. Cover the dough so that the surface does not crust over. Oiled clear film (plastic wrap) placed over the tin or directly on the bread is best. The timing is important as over-rising means the loaf may collapse in the oven, while too little proving will mean the loaf will be heavy and flat.

BELOW: A loaf ready for the final rising.

BELOW: After rising the dough should be double in size – no more.

COOK'S TIP

When stretching dough for baguettes or plaits, work with care so that you don't overstretch it. If the dough feels as if it is going to tear, leave that strand to rest for a minute or two and work on one of the other pieces of dough. When you go back to the first piece, you will find that the gluten has allowed the dough to stretch and you can work it some more.

Proving Baskets

Professional bakers use proving baskets called *bannetons* for baguettes, and circular *couronnes* for round loaves. Some are lined with linen. Proving baskets are available from good kitchenware shops but, depending on the shape you require, you can improvise with baskets and/or earthenware dishes. Simply dust a linen dishtowel liberally with flour and use to line the container.

BELOW: A proving basket will give your loaves a professional finish.

Choosing Tins

Choosing the right size of loaf tin (pan) can be tricky. If it is too small the dough will spill over the top. If it is too large, the final loaf will be uneven. As a rule the tin should be about twice the size of the dough. Professional bakers use black tins, which are considered to be better than shiny metal ones as they absorb the heat better, giving a crisper crust. Always warm a tin before using and then grease it with melted lard (shortening), vegetable oil or unsalted (sweet) butter. Experiment to see what you find most successful. Baking sheets should also be greased to prevent sticking.

TOPPING AND BAKING

The actual baking is perhaps the simplest part of the bread-making process, yet even here the yeast still has a part to play and it is important that you play your part too, by making sure conditions are as ideal as possible. When the loaf goes into the oven the heat kills the yeast, but for the first few minutes, there is a final burst of life and the bread will rise even further before the entire process is set and the air is finally locked in.

PREPARING TO BAKE

While the shaped dough is having its final rise, you will need to preheat the oven to the required temperature. It is important that the oven is at the right temperature when the bread goes in – almost always a hot oven, between 220–230°C/425–450°F/ Gas 7–8, although check the recipe since sweet loaves or those containing a lot of butter cook at a lower temperature. Many recipes suggest that the oven temperature is reduced either immediately after putting the bread in the oven or some time during cooking. This means the bread gets a good blast of heat to start with, and then cooks more gradually. This mimics the original bread ovens, which would have cooled down slowly once the embers had been removed.

SLASHING

Once the loaf is ready for baking, all that is needed is to slash and glaze the loaf. This is done not only for appearance, but also to improve the baking of the loaf. When the loaf goes into the oven, the yeast will continue to produce carbon dioxide for a short time and the loaf will rise. This is called the "spring". Slashing provides escape routes for the gas and gives direction to the spring, so that the loaf will open out around the slashes and retain an even shape. Loaves that have not been allowed enough time to rise will tend to have more spring, and it is therefore important to slash these fairly deeply. If you think your loaf may have over-risen, only slash it gently.

You will also find that some recipes suggest slashing either before the final rising

or some time during it. This will depend on how much you want your loaf to "open up". The earlier it is slashed the more the split will develop. However, unless the recipe specifies otherwise, the general rule is to slash the loaf just before you put it in the oven.

ABOVE: *Cob or coburg – just before baking, slash a deep cross across the top of the loaf.*

ABOVE: *Baguette – slash four or five times on the diagonal just before the baking process.*

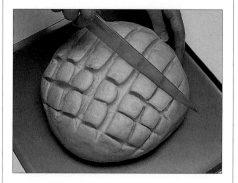

ABOVE: *Porcupine – slashing not only looks attractive, but gives a wonderful crunchy crust to this bread. Make five or six cuts across the bread in one direction, then cut again at right angles, chequerboard fashion.*

ABOVE: *Tin loaf – part-way through rising, make one deep slash along the length of the loaf.*

GLAZING

Glazing has two important functions. It gives an attractive finish to the loaf and it introduces moisture during cooking. This moisture produces steam which also helps to expand the gases in the loaf and ensures it cooks through completely. Glazes also change the consistency and taste of the crust. Bread can be glazed before, during or just after baking: sometimes recipes will suggest all three. If you glaze before and during baking, take care not to brush sticky glazes up to the sides of a tin (pan) or let the glaze drip on to the baking sheet, thereby gluing the bread to its container. This will cause the loaf to crack and rise unevenly.

All sorts of glazes can be used – egg yolk, egg white, milk, butter, sugar solutions, salt solutions and olive oil are regularly used. They also help the toppings to stick to the surface of the loaf.

ABOVE: *Brushing a plait (braid) with beaten egg yolk and milk before baking gives it a golden glaze and a professional-looking finish.*

TOPPINGS

There are as many toppings as there are glazes, if not more, all of which add to the appearance, taste and texture of your finished bread. The dough can be rolled in a topping before the second rising, or it can be glazed and sprinkled with the topping just before baking. Try poppy seeds, grated cheese, caraway seeds, oats, cracked wheat, sea salt, sunflower seeds, sesame seeds, herbs, cornmeal or wheat flakes as alternative toppings.

For basic breads and rolls, toppings are simply a matter of preference – for dinner parties it's always nice to offer people a selection of white and wholemeal rolls, each sprinkled with a different topping. Some breads classically have their own particular topping. *Challah*, for instance, is traditionally sprinkled with poppy seeds, pretzels are covered with sea salt or caraway seeds, while the long thin grissini can be rolled in either sesame or poppy seeds. Rolled oats add a soft texture to loaves, and many traditional British and American loaves, such as

ABOVE: *Roll the dough for a Granary loaf in wheat flakes or cracked wheat.*

ABOVE: *A split tin loaf can be dusted with flour before baking.*

ABOVE: *Grated cheese*

ABOVE: *Cornmeal*

ABOVE: *Cracked wheat*

ABOVE: *Chopped fresh herbs*

ABOVE: *Rolled oats*

ABOVE: *Chopped black olives*

ABOVE: *Poppy seeds*

ABOVE: *Sea salt*

ABOVE: Sesame seeds

ABOVE: Wheat flakes

ABOVE: Sunflower seeds

ABOVE: Caraway seeds

English cottage loaf and San Francisco sourdough bread, have no toppings as such, but a dusting of flour gives an attractive matt sheen to the finished loaf.

Grated cheese and fried onion rings also make more substantial as well as tasty and attractive toppings and many of the Italian breads excel themselves in their rich variety of toppings – whole green or black olives, chunks of sun-dried tomatoes and roasted peppers are frequently added to ciabattas and focaccias. As with glazes, toppings can also be added during and sometimes after cooking. Small breads, such as Vienna rolls, are baked until just golden, brushed with milk or cream and then strewn with sea salt, cumin or caraway seeds. They are then returned to the oven for a few more moments until cooked.

BELOW: For a dinner party or a buffet meal, bake a batch of rolls with assorted toppings.

BAKING TIMES

This will depend on the recipe, the size of the loaf and the heat of the oven. As a general rule, rolls take about 20 minutes, round country breads 40–50 minutes and tin loaves a little longer, 45–60 minutes. To check if bread is ready, remove it from the oven and tap firmly on the base of the loaf with your knuckles. It should have a hollow sound. If it seems soft or does not sound hollow, bake for a little longer.

ABOVE: Check rolls are ready by gently turning one over in a clean dishtowel. The underside should be firm and golden.

ABOVE: To check that a loaf is cooked, tap the base with your knuckles. It should be firm and sound hollow.

ADDING MOISTURE TO THE OVEN

A baker's oven is completely sealed and therefore produces the necessary steam for an evenly risen loaf. At home, glazing helps to produce steam, as does a can of boiling water placed in the bottom of the oven, or you can spray water into the oven two or three times during cooking.

WHAT WENT WRONG

DOUGH WON'T RISE

You may have forgotten the yeast or the yeast may be past its "use-by" date and is dead. To save the dough, make up another batch, making certain the yeast is active. This dough can then be kneaded into the original dough. Alternatively, dissolve the new yeast in warm water and work it into the dough. Another time, always check that yeast is active before adding to flour.

SIDES AND BOTTOM OF BREAD ARE TOO PALE

The oven temperature was too low, or the tin (pan) did not allow heat to penetrate the crust. To remedy this, turn the loaf out of its tin and return it to the oven, placing it upside down on a shelf, for 5–10 minutes.

CRUST TOO SOFT

There was insufficient steam in the oven. You could glaze the crusts before baking next time and spray the inside of the oven with water. Alternatively, place a little hot water in an ovenproof dish in the bottom of the oven during baking. This problem particularly besets French breads and other crusty loaves, which require a certain amount of steam in the oven.

CRUST TOO HARD

Using too much glaze or having too much steam in the oven can harden the crust, so use less glaze next time. To soften a crusty loaf, leave it overnight in a plastic bag.

CRUST SEPARATES FROM THE BREAD

This is caused either by the dough drying out during rising, or by the oven temperature being too low and the dough expanding unevenly. Next time, cover the dough with clear film (plastic wrap) or waxed paper to prevent any moisture loss while rising, and ensure that the oven is preheated to the correct temperature, so that heat penetrates uniformly.

SOFT PALE CRUST

This could be because the bread was not baked for long enough or perhaps the oven temperature was too low. When you think the bread is ready, tap it firmly underneath; it should sound hollow. If it does not, return the bread to the oven, only this time placing it directly on the oven shelf.

LOAF IS CRUMBLY AND DRY

Either the bread was baked for too long or you used too much flour. Next time check the quantities in the recipe. It is also possible that the oven was too hot. Next time reduce the temperature and check the loaf when the crust looks golden brown.

LARGE HOLES IN LOAF

Either the dough was not knocked back (punched down) properly before shaping or it was not kneaded enough originally.

BREAD HAS A YEASTY FLAVOUR

Too much yeast was used. If doubling recipe quantities, do not double the amount of yeast but use one and a half times the amount. In addition, do not overcompensate for a cool room by adding extra yeast unless you don't mind a yeasty flavour. Wait a little longer instead – the bread will rise in the end.

LOAF COLLAPSES IN THE OVEN

Either the wrong flour was used for a particular recipe or the dough was left too long for the second rising and has over-risen. As a rule, the dough should only double in bulk.

LOAF IS DENSE AND FLAT

Too much liquid was used and the dough has become too soft, or was not kneaded enough. Always check the recipe for quantities of liquid needed until you are confident about judging the consistency of the dough. The dough should be kneaded firmly for at least 10 minutes.

BREAD-MAKING MACHINES

Bread makers may take the fun out of bread making, but if you enjoy home-made bread on a daily basis, they make it an incredibly easy process. All you need to do is add the correct ingredients, press the right buttons and – hey presto – a few hours later, you have a freshly cooked loaf of bread!

Many bread makers have a timer switch, so that you can programme your bread to be ready for when you get up in the morning. Almost all bread makers will make a variety of different types and sizes of loaves, and many have a feature where the bread maker does the kneading and rising, with the baking up to you – useful for French loaves, pizzas or any other breads that are not a standard loaf shape.

THINGS TO LOOK OUT FOR WHEN BUYING A BREAD-MAKING MACHINE

♦ Unless you are likely to need only one small loaf a day, choose a machine with the option of making small, medium and large loaves.

♦ "Rapid-bake": this cuts down on resting time, and by recommending extra yeast, also cuts down on rising. You will get a loaf in under 2 hours.

♦ Dough (or manual) cycle: allows you to remove the dough prior to shaping when making loaves that are not the standard "loaf" shape.

♦ Crust colour: some bread makers have the option of a dark, medium or pale crust.

♦ Sweet bread cycle: breads that are high in sugar or fat need to bake at slightly lower temperatures, otherwise these ingredients tend to burn. A sweet bread cycle means that the bread-making machine will automatically adjust the heat to allow for this, if programmed to do so first.

♦ Timer feature: this useful feature allows you to set the bread maker so that the bread is ready for when you get up in the morning or when the children come home from school.

USING A BREAD MAKER

1 Add the easy-blend or fast-action yeast to the bread tin (pan). If you are making a quick or rapid-bake loaf, you may need to add up to one and a half times the usual quantity of yeast, but check the manufacturer's recommendation.

2 Add the remaining ingredients to the bread tin and place in the machine. Select the type of loaf you wish to bake, the size and colour of the crust.

3 Dried fruit, olives or other ingredients used to flavour breads are added after the initial kneading. This is to ensure that they are not broken up too much. Depending on the type of loaf you choose to make, your bread will be ready to eat in 2–5 hours.

TIPS FOR CONVERTING RECIPES

Once you're familiar with your bread machine and confident using suggested recipes, you will probably want to adapt some of your own favourite recipes. A loaf baked in a bread-making machine will, of course, always be "loaf-shaped", but since most bread makers have a dough cycle (where the dough is kneaded but not baked), it is possible to prepare rolls, ciabatta and baguettes – indeed most breads featured in this book. It is important that you reduce the recipe according to the maximum capacity of your machine (and even further if you wish to make a small loaf).

Make sure that the proportions of all the essential ingredients for the recipe are approximately as follows:

FOR A 450G/1LB LOAF
Flour: 225–300g/8–11oz/2–2¾ cups
Liquid (water or milk):
180–250ml/6–8fl oz/¾–1 cup
Salt: 1.5–5ml/¼–1 tsp
Fat: 10–45ml/2 tsp–3 tbsp
Salt: 10–45ml/2 tsp–3 tbsp
Dried yeast: 7–15ml/1½ tsp–1 tbsp
FOR A 675G/1½LB LOAF
Flour: 350–450g/12–16oz/3–4 cups
Liquid (water or milk):
250–300ml/8–10fl oz/1–1¼ cups
Salt: 2.5–7.5ml/½–1½ tsp
Fat: 15–60ml/1–4 tbsp
Salt: 15–60ml/1–4 tbsp
Dried yeast: 7–15ml/1½ tsp–1 tbsp

♦ If adding fruit or other ingredients, reduce the quantities proportionately.

♦ Always use a fast-action yeast.

♦ If adding eggs, remember that one large egg is roughly equal to 60ml/4 tbsp liquid, so reduce the liquid accordingly.

♦ When adapting a recipe, monitor the machine carefully and make a note of any adjustments you may need to make. For instance, pay attention to whether the mixture is too moist or whether the machine struggles to knead the dough. If the loaf is too tall, this may be because you've added too much liquid, yeast or sugar, or added insufficient salt.

BREAD-MAKING EQUIPMENT

Bread making is not an exact science and you do not need a fully equipped kitchen with state-of-the-art utensils if you decide to have a go. In the long run, though, you may decide that some things are essential and others could be useful.

SCALES/WEIGHTS
Balance scales are more accurate but spring balance scales are easier to use and more convenient (especially if you have a tendency to lose the weights). Bear in mind, if buying scales for bread making, that you will probably be using large quantities of flours and will therefore need large-size scales with a deep basin.

MEASURING JUGS (CUPS)
Heatproof glass jugs are most convenient as liquids can safely be heated in them in

BELOW: Be sure to get scales with a large measuring bowl.

the microwave and they are dishwasher safe. Measurements should be clearly marked on the outside; be sure to buy jugs with both imperial and metric measurements so that you can follow any recipe with ease.

MEASURING SPOONS
These are always useful in the kitchen for adding small quantities of spices etc. A set of spoons measures from 1.5ml/¼ tsp to 15ml/1 tbsp.

FOOD PROCESSOR
Most food processors can mix and knead dough extremely efficiently and in a fraction of the time it would take by hand. Always check the instruction book about bread making since only the larger machines can handle large amounts of dough, and you may find that it is necessary to knead the dough in batches.

FOOD MIXER
An electric mixer fitted with a dough hook will knead dough in a time similar to that taken to knead by hand but with much less effort. Small machines can cope with only small amounts of dough and if you are considering buying a machine for bread-making purposes, make sure that the equipment is suitable for the quantities of bread you are likely to want to make.

SIEVES
Some finer breads may require the flour to be sifted so it is worth having at least one large sieve for flours and a smaller sieve for adding ground spices or dusting the loaves with flour or icing (confectioners') sugar after baking them.

LEFT: Sieves for flour or spices

ABOVE: A selection of glass bowls

BOWLS

If you have not got a selection already, it is worth buying some now since it is not possible to make bread (at least in the kitchen) without at least two good-sized bowls. Choose a bowl with a wide mouth, which is still deep enough to contain the batter or dough. A smaller bowl is also useful (although you can use the measuring jug or cup) for making up dried yeast.

ROLLING PIN

Some doughs need to be rolled out and you will need a large rolling pin for this job. A wooden rolling pin that is long and smooth and has no separate handles is ideal for bread making.

DOUGH KNIFE OR SCRAPER

This is extremely handy when kneading dough by hand. The rectangular piece of steel on a wooden handle is particularly useful in the early part of kneading, for lifting and working sticky or difficult doughs. The blades normally measure about 10 × 13cm/4 × 5in and should ideally be slightly flexible rather than rigid.

COOK'S KNIFE

You will need a sharp knife for slashing the dough – either during rising or just before baking. Some recipe books suggest using a razor for this job but the blade does need to be very sharp indeed. Since a good cook's knife can be kept in razor-sharp condition, this is the preferable option and adds a professional touch to your loaves.

ABOVE: Bread knife and cook's knife

LEFT: Dough knife/scraper

ABOVE: Rolling pin

ABOVE: Pastry brushes

BREAD KNIFE

A dull knife can wreak havoc on a fresh loaf of bread, so make sure you use a good bread knife. Bread should be cut in a saw-ing motion, which is why bread knives have long serrated blades. A plain cook's knife, although it will cut through the bread, will spoil the tex-ture of the crumb.

PASTRY BRUSH

This is essential for glazing loaves and rolls. Choose a good, wide brush. It is worth spending extra for a brush that will not lose its bristles. Use a brush made from natural fibres; nylon will melt if used for brushing hot loaves during cooking.

BREAD TINS

Bread tins (pans) come in all sizes and it is worth having a selection. Include a 450g/1lb and preferably two 1kg/2¼ lb tins so that you can make loaves in a variety of shapes and sizes. If the tins are labelled with their dimensions, rather than their

BELOW: Shallow loaf and cake tins

capacity, look out for 18 × 7.5cm/7 × 3in (equivalent to 450g/1lb) and 23 × 13cm/9 × 5in (equivalent to 1kg/2¼ lb). Other use-ful sizes are 30 × 10cm/12 × 4in and 25 × 10cm/10 × 4in. Professional bakers prefer matt black tins, which absorb the heat better than the shiny ones and there-fore make the crust crisper. The wider

ABOVE: High-sided loaf tins

shallow tins are mostly used for fruit breads. Tin loaves are baked in plain, high-sided tins; farmhouse loaves are slightly shallower and tins may be stamped with the word "Farmhouse". Cake tins (pans) are sometimes used for bread making. Monkey bread, for instance, is baked in a 23cm/9in springform ring cake tin, while buchty – breakfast rolls that are batch-baked – require a square, loose-bottomed cake tin with straight sides that will support the rolls as they rise.

Several speciality breads are baked in a deep 15cm/6in cake tin. These breads include *panettone* and Sally Lunn.

If you are fond of baking focaccia, you will find a 25cm/10in pizza pan or shallow round cake tin invaluable.

MOULDS

There are various sizes of brioche mould for the traditional fluted brioche, including individual bun size. A *kugelhopf* mould is a fluted ring mould essential for making the Alsace or German *kugel-hopf* or the Viennese *gugelhupf*. A savarin mould is a straight-sided ring mould for

savarins and other ring-shaped breads. If you don't have the correct mould, it is sometimes possible to improvise. Boston brown bread, for instance, can be baked in a special mould, but the heatproof glass jar from a cafetière coffee jug (carafe) can be used instead, or even two 450g/1lb coffee cans, without the lids, work perfectly well once washed and dried.

BELOW: Baking sheets and patty tins

BAKING SHEETS
When buying baking sheets, look for ones that are either completely flat, or have a lip only on one long edge. This makes it easier to slide bread or rolls on to a wire rack. Strong, heavy baking sheets distribute the heat evenly.

MUFFIN TINS AND PATTY TINS
Muffin tins (pans) with 7.5cm/3in cups are very useful for making elaborately shaped rolls like the New England Fantans, while the larger patty tins and Yorkshire

pudding tins come into their own for specialities like Georgian Khachapuri. The tins support the dough while it is filled with cheese and then tied into a topknot.

FLOWER POTS
Earthenware flower pots can also be used for baking. These need to be tempered before being used for bread. Brush the

new, perfectly clean pots liberally inside and out with oil and place in a hot oven (about 200°C/400°F/Gas 6) for about 30 minutes. (This can conveniently be done while you are cooking something else.) Do this several times until the pots are impregnated with oil. They can then be used for baking bread and will need very little greasing.

BELOW: Earthenware flower pots make unusual moulds for loaves.

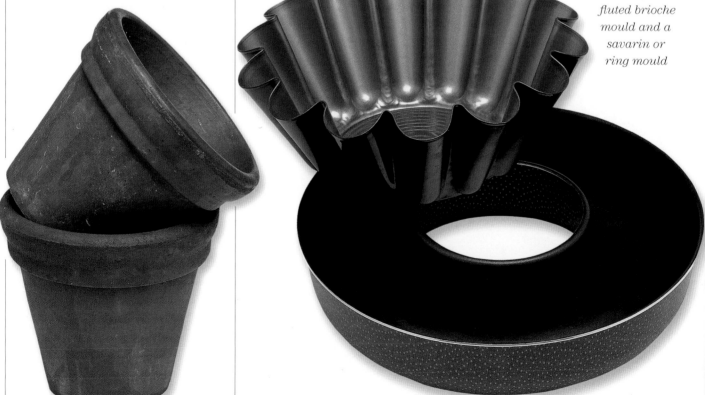

LEFT: A French fluted brioche mould and a savarin or ring mould

LONGUETS

Longuets are moulded pieces of steel, like corrugated iron, used for baking baguettes. They are designed with the professional baker in mind and are unlikely to be suitable for an average size oven.

BAKING STONE

Baking stones are now widely available, sold principally for pizzas but also useful for making thick crusted loaves. They are the nearest thing to replicating an authentic brick-floored oven. The stones are heated in the oven and then the bread is placed on top.

BANNETONS AND COURONNES

These are the canvas-lined proving baskets used by French bakers for their bread: *bannetons* are used for baguettes, *couronnes* for round loaves. In Germany, sourdough bread is sometimes proved in a floured basket, which has the effect of creating a crust that looks like wicker.

GRIDDLE

This is a heavy cast-iron pan used on top of the stove for griddle cakes, soda farls, bannocks and even Indian breads like missi rotis and chapatis. Weight is the important feature with griddles, so that heat can be evenly dispersed.

Griddles can have handles or have the more old-fashioned design of a hooped handle over the entire pan, often with a small hoop in the centre which would have been used to hang the griddle over a peat fire. In Scotland, where they are still widely used, griddles are also known as girdles.

Square-shaped griddles that come with metal hoops for muffins and crumpets are also available in good kitchen stores. The hoops have a diameter of about 10cm/4in and are about 2.5cm/1in deep.

BELOW: This short, deep banneton is ideal for shorter French loaves.

ABOVE: Very long bannetons are designed for supporting baguettes during the final rising.

BELOW: A griddle for pikelets and other free form breads, such as griddle-baked soda bread and oatcakes.

BREAD RECIPES OF THE WORLD

There are few things more pleasurable than the aroma and taste of freshly cooked home-made bread. This collection of recipes includes savoury and sweet classics from around the world, as well as a good selection of lesser-known specialities. A wide variety of flours, all of which are readily available, has been used to create distinctive breads which reflect the different flavours of each region. These recipes aim to take the mystery out of bread making and inspire you to try baking many different and delicious breads.

GRANARY COB

450g/1lb/4 cups Granary (whole-wheat) or malthouse flour
10ml/2 tsp salt
15g/½ oz fresh yeast
300ml/½ pint/1¼ cups lukewarm water or milk and water mixed

FOR THE TOPPING
30ml/2 tbsp water
2.5ml/½ tsp salt
wheat flakes or cracked wheat, to sprinkle

MAKES 1 ROUND LOAF

Cob is an old word meaning "head". If you make a slash across the top of the dough, the finished loaf, known as a Danish cob, will look like a large roll. A Coburg cob has a cross cut in the top before baking.

1 Lightly flour a baking sheet. Sift the flour and salt together in a large bowl and make a well in the centre. Place in a very low oven for 5 minutes to warm.

2 Mix the yeast with a little of the water or milk mixture then blend in the rest. Add the yeast mixture to the centre of the flour and mix to a dough.

3 Turn out on to a floured surface. Knead for 10 minutes until smooth and elastic. Place in a lightly oiled bowl, cover with oiled clear film (plastic wrap) and leave to rise, in a warm place, for 1¼ hours, or until doubled in bulk.

4 Turn the dough out on to a lightly floured surface and knock back (punch down). Knead for 2–3 minutes, then roll into a ball, making sure the dough looks like a plump round cushion, otherwise it will become too flat. Place in the centre of the prepared baking sheet. Cover with an inverted bowl and leave to rise, in a warm place, for 30–45 minutes.

5 Mix the water and salt and brush over the bread. Sprinkle with wheat flakes or cracked wheat.

6 Meanwhile, preheat the oven to 230°C/450°F/Gas 8. Bake for 15 minutes, then reduce the oven temperature to 200°C/400°F/Gas 6 and bake for a further 20 minutes, or until the loaf is firm to the touch and sounds hollow when tapped on the base. Cool on a wire rack.

EASY WHOLEMEAL LOAVES

This quick and easy recipe is wonderfully simple to make – the dough requires no kneading and takes only a minute to mix. The loaves should keep moist for several days.

1 Grease three loaf tins (pans), each about 21 × 11 × 6cm/8½ × 4½ × 2½ in and set aside in a warm place. Sift the flour and salt together in a large bowl and warm slightly to take off the chill.

2 Sprinkle the dried yeast over 150ml/¼ pint/⅔ cup of the water. After a couple of minutes stir in the sugar. Leave for 10 minutes.

3 Make a well in the centre of the flour and stir in the yeast mixture and remaining water. The dough should be slippery. Mix for about 1 minute, working the sides into the middle.

4 Divide among the tins, cover with oiled clear film (plastic wrap) and leave in a warm place, for 30 minutes, or until the dough has risen by about a third to within 1cm/½ in of the top of the tins.

1.4kg/3lb/12 cups wholemeal (whole-wheat) bread flour
15ml/1 tbsp salt
15ml/1 tbsp easy-blend (rapid-rise) dried yeast
1.2 litres/2 pints/5 cups lukewarm water
15ml/1 tbsp muscovado (molasses) sugar

MAKES 3 LOAVES

COOK'S TIP
Muscovado sugar gives this bread a rich flavour. An unrefined cane sugar, it is dark and moist.

5 Meanwhile, preheat the oven to 200°C/400°F/Gas 6. Bake for 40 minutes, or until the loaves are crisp and sound hollow when tapped on the base. Turn out on to a wire rack to cool.

POPPY-SEEDED BLOOMER

This satisfying white bread, which is the British version of the chunky baton loaf found throughout Europe, is made by a slower rising method and with less yeast than usual. It produces a longer-keeping loaf with a fuller flavour. The dough takes about 8 hours to rise, so you'll need to start this bread early in the morning.

675g/1½ lb/6 cups unbleached white bread flour
10ml/2 tsp salt
15g/½ oz fresh yeast
430ml/15fl oz/1⅞ cups water

FOR THE TOPPING
2.5ml/½ tsp salt
30ml/2 tbsp water
poppy seeds, for sprinkling

MAKES 1 LARGE LOAF

1 Lightly grease a baking sheet. Sift the flour and salt together into a large bowl and make a well in the centre.

2 Mix the yeast and 150ml/¼ pint/⅔ cup of the water in a jug (pitcher) or bowl. Mix in the remaining water. Add to the centre of the flour. Mix, gradually incorporating the surrounding flour, until the mixture forms a firm dough.

COOK'S TIP
The traditional cracked, crusty appearance of this loaf is difficult to achieve in a domestic oven. However, you can get a similar result by spraying the oven with water before baking. If the underneath of the loaf is not very crusty at the end of baking, turn the loaf over on the baking sheet, switch off the heat and leave in the oven for a further 5–10 minutes.

VARIATION
For a more rustic loaf, replace up to half the flour with wholemeal (whole-wheat) bread flour.

3 Turn out on to a lightly floured surface and knead the dough very well, for at least 10 minutes, until smooth and elastic. Place in a lightly oiled bowl, cover with lightly oiled clear film (plastic wrap) and leave at cool room temperature, about 15–18°C/60–65°F, for 5–6 hours, or until doubled in bulk.

4 Knock back (punch down) the dough, turn out on to a lightly floured surface and knead it thoroughly and quite hard for about 5 minutes. Return the dough to the bowl, and re-cover. Leave to rise, at cool room temperature, for a further 2 hours or slightly longer.

5 Knock back again and repeat the thorough kneading. Leave the dough to rest for 5 minutes, then roll out on a lightly floured surface into a rectangle 2.5cm/1in thick. Roll the dough up from one long side and shape it into a square-ended thick baton shape about 33 × 13cm/13 × 5in.

6 Place it seam side up on a lightly floured baking sheet, cover and leave to rest for 15 minutes. Turn the loaf over and place on the greased baking sheet. Plump up by tucking the dough under the sides and ends. Using a sharp knife, cut 6 diagonal slashes on the top.

7 Leave to rest, covered, in a warm place, for 10 minutes. Meanwhile preheat the oven to 230°C/450°F/Gas 8.

8 Mix the salt and water together and brush this glaze over the bread. Sprinkle with poppy seeds.

9 Spray the oven with water, bake the bread immediately for 20 minutes, then reduce the oven temperature to 200°C/400°F/Gas 6; bake for 25 minutes more, or until golden. Transfer to a wire rack to cool.

COTTAGE LOAF

675g/1½ lb/6 cups unbleached white bread flour
10ml/2 tsp salt
20g/¾ oz fresh yeast
400ml/14fl oz/1⅔ cups lukewarm water

MAKES 1 LARGE ROUND LOAF

COOK'S TIPS
• To ensure a good-shaped cottage loaf the dough needs to be firm enough to support the weight of the top ball.
• Do not over-prove the dough on the second rising or the loaf may topple over – but even if it does it will still taste good.

Snipping the top and bottom sections of the dough at 5cm/2in intervals not only looks good but also helps the loaf to expand in the oven.

1 Lightly grease two baking sheets. Sift the flour and salt together into a large bowl and make a well in the centre.

2 Mix the yeast in 150ml/¼ pint/⅔ cup of the water until dissolved. Pour into the centre of the flour with the remaining water and mix to a firm dough.

3 Knead on a lightly floured surface for 10 minutes until smooth and elastic. Place in a lightly oiled bowl, cover with lightly oiled clear film (plastic wrap) and leave to rise, in a warm place, for about 1 hour, or until doubled in bulk.

4 Turn out on to a lightly floured surface and knock back (punch down). Knead for 2–3 minutes then divide into two-thirds and one-third; shape each to a ball.

5 Place the balls of dough on the prepared baking sheets. Cover with inverted bowls and leave to rise, in a warm place, for about 30 minutes (see Cook's Tips).

6 Gently flatten the top of the larger round of dough and, with a sharp knife, cut a cross in the centre, about 4cm/1½ in across. Brush with a little water and place the smaller round on top.

7 Carefully press a hole through the middle of the top ball, down into the lower part, using your thumb and first two fingers of one hand. Cover with lightly oiled clear film and leave to rest in a warm place for about 10 minutes. Preheat the oven to 220°C/425°F/Gas 7 and place the bread on the lower shelf. It will finish expanding as the oven heats up. Bake for 35–40 minutes, or until golden brown and sounding hollow when tapped. Cool on a wire rack.

SCOTTISH MORNING ROLLS

These rolls are best served warm, as soon as they are baked. In Scotland they are a firm favourite for breakfast with a fried egg and bacon.

450g/1lb/4 cups unbleached plain (all-purpose) white flour, plus extra for dusting
10ml/2 tsp salt
20g/¾ oz fresh yeast
150ml/¼ pint/⅔ cup lukewarm milk
150ml/¼ pint/⅔ cup lukewarm water
30ml/2 tbsp milk, for glazing

MAKES 10 ROLLS

1 Grease two baking sheets. Sift the flour and salt together into a large bowl and make a well in the centre. Mix the yeast with the milk, then mix in the water. Add to the centre of the flour and mix together to form a soft dough.

2 Knead the dough lightly in the bowl, then cover with lightly oiled clear film (plastic wrap) and leave in a warm place, for 1 hour, or until doubled in bulk. Turn the dough out on to a lightly floured surface and knock back (punch down).

3 Divide the dough into 10 equal pieces. Knead lightly and, using a rolling pin, shape each piece to a flat oval 10 × 7.5cm/4 × 3in or a flat round 9cm/3½ in.

4 Transfer to the prepared baking sheets, spaced well apart, and cover with oiled clear film. Leave to rise, in a warm place, for about 30 minutes.

5 Meanwhile, preheat the oven to 200°C/400°F/Gas 6. Press each roll in the centre with the three middle fingers to equalise the air bubbles and to help prevent blistering. Brush with milk and dust with flour. Bake for 15–20 minutes or until lightly browned. Dust with more flour and cool slightly on a wire rack. Serve warm.

SPLIT TIN

*500g/1¼ lb/5 cups unbleached white
bread flour, plus extra for dusting
10ml/2 tsp salt
15g/½ oz fresh yeast
300ml/½ pint/1¼ cups lukewarm
water
60ml/4 tbsp lukewarm milk*

MAKES 1 LOAF

*As its name suggests, this homely loaf is so called because of the centre split.
Some bakers mould the dough in two loaves – they join together whilst
proving but retain the characteristic crack after baking.*

1 Lightly grease a 900g/2lb loaf tin (pan) (18.5 × 11.5cm/7¼ × 4½in). Sift the flour and salt together into a large bowl and make a well in the centre. Mix the yeast with half the lukewarm water in a jug (pitcher), then stir in the remaining water.

2 Pour the yeast mixture into the centre of the flour and using your fingers, mix in a little flour. Gradually mix in more of the flour from around the edge of the bowl to form a thick, smooth batter.

3 Sprinkle a little more flour from around the edge over the batter and leave in a warm place to "sponge". Bubbles will appear in the batter after about 20 minutes. Add the milk and remaining flour; mix to a firm dough.

4 Place on a lightly floured surface and knead for about 10 minutes until smooth and elastic. Place in a lightly oiled bowl, cover with oiled clear film (plastic wrap) and leave in a warm place, for 1–1¼ hours, or until nearly doubled in bulk.

5 Knock back (punch down) the dough and turn out on to a lightly floured surface. Shape it into a rectangle, the length of the tin. Roll up lengthways, tuck the ends under and place seam side down in the prepared tin. Cover and leave to rise, in a warm place, for about 20–30 minutes, or until nearly doubled in bulk.

6 Using a sharp knife, make one deep central slash the length of the bread; dust with flour. Leave for 10–15 minutes.

7 Meanwhile, preheat the oven to 230°C/450°F/Gas 8. Bake for 15 minutes, then reduce the oven temperature to 200°C/400°F/Gas 6. Bake for 20–25 minutes more, or until the bread is golden and sounds hollow when tapped on the base. Turn out on to a wire rack to cool.

WELSH BARA BRITH

20g/¾ oz fresh yeast
210ml/7fl oz/scant 1 cup lukewarm milk
450g/1lb/4 cups unbleached white
bread flour
75g/3oz/6 tbsp butter or lard
(shortening)
5ml/1 tsp mixed (apple pie) spice
2.5ml/½ tsp salt
50g/2oz/⅓ cup light brown sugar
1 egg, lightly beaten
115g/4oz/⅔ cup seedless raisins,
slightly warmed
75g/3oz/scant ½ cup currants,
slightly warmed
40g/1½ oz/¼ cup mixed chopped
(candied) peel
15–30ml/1–2 tbsp clear honey,
for glazing

MAKES 1 LARGE ROUND LOAF

This rich, fruity bread – the name literally means "speckled bread" – is a speciality from North Wales. The honey glaze makes a delicious topping.

1 Grease a baking sheet. Blend the yeast with a little of the milk, then stir in the remainder. Set aside for 10 minutes.

2 Sift the flour into a large bowl and rub in the butter or lard until the mixture resembles breadcrumbs. Stir in the mixed spice, salt and sugar and make a well in the centre.

3 Add the yeast mixture and beaten egg to the centre of the flour and mix to a rough dough.

4 Turn out the dough on to a lightly floured surface and knead for about 10 minutes until smooth and elastic. Place in a lightly oiled bowl, cover with lightly oiled clear film (plastic wrap) and leave to rise, in a warm place, for 1½ hours, or until doubled in bulk.

5 Turn out on to a lightly floured surface, knock back (punch down), and knead in the dried fruits and peel. Shape into a round and place on the baking sheet. Cover with oiled clear film and leave to rise, in a warm place, for 1 hour, or until the dough doubles in size.

6 Meanwhile, preheat the oven to 200°C/400°F/Gas 6. Bake for 30 minutes or until the bread sounds hollow when tapped on the base. If the bread starts to over-brown, cover it loosely with foil for the last 10 minutes. Transfer the bread to a wire rack, brush with honey and leave to cool.

VARIATIONS
• The bara brith can be baked in a 1.5–1.75 litre/2½–3 pint/6¼–7½ cup loaf tin (pan) or deep round or square cake tin (pan), if you prefer.
• For a more wholesome loaf, replace half the white flour with wholemeal (whole-wheat) bread flour.

SHAPED DINNER ROLLS

These professional-looking rolls are perfect for entertaining. You can always make double the amount of dough and freeze half, tightly wrapped. Just thaw, glaze and bake as required.

450g/1lb/4 cups unbleached white bread flour
10ml/2 tsp salt
2.5ml/½ tsp caster (superfine) sugar
6g/¼oz sachet easy-blend (rapid-rise) dried yeast
50g/2oz/¼ cup butter or margarine
250ml/8fl oz/1 cup lukewarm milk
1 egg

FOR THE TOPPING
1 egg yolk
15ml/1 tbsp water
poppy seeds and sesame seeds

MAKES 12 ROLLS

5 *To make trefoils:* divide each piece of dough into three and roll into balls. Place the three balls together in a triangular shape.

6 *To make batons:* shape each piece of dough into an oblong and slash the surface of each with diagonal cuts just before baking.

7 *To make cottage rolls:* divide each piece of dough into two-thirds and one-third and shape into rounds. Place the small one on top of the large one and make a hole through the centre with the handle of a wooden spoon.

8 *To make knots:* shape each piece of dough into a long roll and tie a single knot, pulling the ends through.

9 Place the dinner rolls on the prepared baking sheets, spacing them well apart, cover the rolls with oiled clear film and leave to rise, in a warm place, for about 30 minutes, or until doubled in bulk.

10 Meanwhile, preheat the oven to 220°C/425°F/Gas 7. Mix the egg yolk and water together for the glaze and brush over the rolls. Sprinkle some with poppy seeds and some with sesame seeds. Bake for 15–18 minutes or until golden. Lift the rolls off the sheet using a metal spatula and transfer to a wire rack to cool.

1 Lightly grease two baking sheets. Sift the flour and salt into a large bowl and stir in the sugar and yeast. Add the butter or margarine and rub in until the mixture resembles fine breadcrumbs.

3 Turn the dough out on to a lightly floured surface, knock back (punch down) and knead for 2–3 minutes. Divide the dough into 12 equal pieces and shape into rolls as described in steps 4–8.

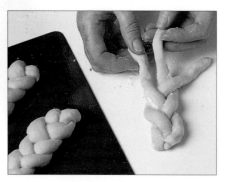

2 Make a well in the centre. Add the milk and egg to the well and mix to a dough. Knead on a floured surface for 10 minutes until smooth and elastic. Place in a lightly oiled bowl, cover with lightly oiled clear film (plastic wrap) and leave to rise, in a warm place, for 1 hour, or until doubled in bulk.

4 *To make braids:* divide each piece of dough into three equal pieces. Working on a lightly floured surface, roll each piece to a sausage, keeping the lengths and widths even. Pinch three strips together at one end, then braid them neatly but not too tightly. Pinch the ends together and tuck under the braid.

IRISH SODA BREAD

*225g/8oz/2 cups unbleached
plain (all-purpose) flour
225g/8oz/2 cups wholemeal (whole-
wheat) flour, plus extra for dusting
5ml/1 tsp salt
10ml/2 tsp bicarbonate of soda
(baking soda)
10ml/2 tsp cream of tartar
40g/1½ oz/3 tbsp butter or lard (shortening)
5ml/1 tsp caster (superfine) sugar
350–375ml/12–13fl oz/1½–1⅔ cups
buttermilk*

MAKES 1 ROUND LOAF

VARIATION
Shape into two small loaves and bake
for 25–30 minutes.

*Soda bread can be prepared in minutes and is excellent served warm, fresh
from the oven. You can use all plain white flour, if preferred, to create a bread
with a finer texture.*

1 Preheat the oven to 190°C/375°F/Gas 5.
Lightly grease a baking sheet. Sift the
flour and salt into a large bowl.

2 Add the bicarbonate of soda and
cream of tartar, then rub in the butter or
lard. Stir in the sugar.

3 Pour in sufficient buttermilk to mix to
a soft dough. Do not over-mix or the
bread will be heavy and tough. Shape
into a round on a lightly floured surface.

4 Place on the prepared baking sheet
and mark a cross using a sharp knife,
cutting deep into the dough.

5 Dust lightly with wholemeal flour and
bake for 35–45 minutes or until well
risen and the bread sounds hollow when
tapped on the base. Serve warm.

CRUMPETS

225g/8oz/2 cups unbleached plain
(all-purpose) flour
225g/8oz/2 cups unbleached white
bread flour
10ml/2 tsp salt
600ml/1 pint/2½ cups milk and
water mixed
30ml/2 tbsp sunflower oil
15ml/1 tbsp caster (superfine) sugar
15g/½ oz fresh yeast
2.5ml/½ tsp bicarbonate of soda
(baking soda)
120ml/4fl oz/½ cup lukewarm water

MAKES ABOUT 20 CRUMPETS

COOK'S TIP
If the batter does not produce the
characteristic bubbles, add a little
more water before cooking the next
batch of crumpets.

*Home-made crumpets are less doughy and not as heavy as most supermarket
versions. Serve them lightly toasted, oozing with butter.*

1 Lightly grease a griddle or heavy frying
pan and 4 × 8cm/3¼ in plain pastry
(cookie) cutters or crumpet rings.

2 Sift the flours and salt together into a
large bowl and make a well in the
centre. Heat the milk and water
mixture, oil and sugar until lukewarm.
Mix the yeast with 150ml/¼ pint/⅔ cup
of this liquid.

3 Add the yeast mixture and remaining
liquid to the centre of the flour and beat
vigorously for about 5 minutes until
smooth and elastic. Cover with oiled
clear film (plastic wrap) and leave in a
warm place, for about 1½ hours, or until
the mixture is bubbly and about to fall.

4 Dissolve the soda in the lukewarm
water and stir into the batter. Re-cover
and leave to rise for 30 minutes.

5 Place the cutters or crumpet rings on
the griddle and warm over a medium
heat. Fill the cutters or rings a generous
1cm/½ in deep. Cook over a gentle heat
for 6–7 minutes. The tops should be
dry, with a mass of tiny holes.

6 Carefully remove the cutters or rings
and turn the crumpets over. Cook for
1–2 minutes or until pale golden. Repeat
with remaining batter. Serve warm.

ENGLISH MUFFINS

450g/1lb/4 cups unbleached white
bread flour
7.5ml/1½ tsp salt
350–375ml/12–13fl oz/1½–1⅔ cups
lukewarm milk
2.5ml/½ tsp caster (superfine) sugar
15g/½oz fresh yeast
15ml/1 tbsp melted butter or olive oil
rice flour or semolina, for dusting

MAKES 9 MUFFINS

COOK'S TIPS
• Muffins should be cut around the
outer edge only using a sharp knife
and then torn apart. If toasting, toast
the whole muffins first and then split
them in half.
• If you'd like to serve the muffins
warm, transfer them to a wire rack to
cool slightly before serving.

*Perfect served warm, split open and buttered for afternoon tea; or try these
favourites toasted, split and topped with ham and eggs for brunch.*

1 Generously flour a non-stick baking
sheet. Very lightly grease a griddle. Sift
the flour and salt together into a large
bowl and make a well in the centre.
Blend 150ml/¼ pint/⅔ cup of the milk,
sugar and yeast together. Stir in the
remaining milk and butter or oil.

2 Add the yeast mixture to the centre of
the flour and beat for 4–5 minutes until
smooth and elastic. The dough will be
soft but just hold its shape. Cover with
lightly oiled clear film (plastic wrap) and
leave to rise, in a warm place, for 45–60
minutes, or until doubled in bulk.

3 Turn out on a floured surface and
knock back (punch down). Roll out to
1cm/½ in thick. Using a floured 7.5cm/3in
plain cutter, cut out nine rounds.

4 Dust with rice flour or semolina and
place on the prepared baking sheet.
Cover and leave to rise, in a warm place,
for about 20–30 minutes.

5 Warm the griddle over a medium heat.
Carefully transfer the muffins in batches
to the griddle. Cook slowly for about
7 minutes on each side or until golden
brown. Transfer to a wire rack to cool.

FRENCH BAGUETTES

500g/1¹/₄ lb/5 cups unbleached white
bread flour
115g/4oz/1 cup fine French plain
(all-purpose) flour
10ml/2 tsp salt
15g/¹/₂ oz fresh yeast
525ml/18fl oz/2¹/₄ cups lukewarm
water

MAKES 3 LOAVES

VARIATION

If you make baguettes regularly you
may want to purchase baguette
frames to hold and bake the breads
in, or long *bannetons* in which to
prove this wonderful bread.

Baguettes are difficult to reproduce at home as they require a very hot oven
and steam. However, by using less yeast and a triple fermentation you can
produce a bread with a superior taste and far better texture than mass-
produced baguettes. These are best eaten on the day of baking.

1 Sift the flours and salt into a large bowl.
Add the yeast to the water in another
bowl and stir to dissolve. Gradually beat
in half the flour mixture to form a batter.
Cover with clear film (plastic wrap) and
leave at room temperature for about
3 hours, or until nearly trebled in size
and starting to collapse.

2 Add the remaining flour a little at a
time, beating with your hand. Turn out
on to a lightly floured surface and knead
for 8–10 minutes to form a moist dough.
Place in a lightly oiled bowl, cover with
lightly oiled clear film and leave to rise,
in a warm place, for about 1 hour.

3 When the dough has almost doubled in
bulk, knock it back (punch it down),
turn out on to a lightly floured surface
and divide into three equal pieces. Shape
each into a ball and then into a rectangle
measuring about 15 × 7.5cm/6 × 3in.

4 Fold the bottom third up lengthways
and the top third down and press down
to make sure the pieces of dough are in
contact. Seal the edges. Repeat two or
three more times until each loaf is an
oblong. Leave to rest in between folding
for a few minutes, if necessary, to avoid
tearing the dough.

5 Gently stretch each piece of dough
lengthways into a 33–35cm/13–14in
long loaf. Pleat a floured dishtowel on a
baking sheet to make three moulds for
the loaves. Place the breads between
the pleats of the towel, to help hold
their shape while rising. Cover with
lightly oiled clear film and leave to rise,
in a warm place, for 45–60 minutes.

6 Meanwhile, preheat the oven to
maximum, at least 230°C/450°F/Gas 8.
Roll the loaves on to a baking sheet,
spaced well apart. Using a sharp knife,
slash the top of each loaf several times
with long diagonal slits. Place at the top
of the oven, spray the inside of the oven
with water and bake for 20–25 minutes,
or until golden. Spray the oven twice
more during the first 5 minutes of
baking. Transfer to a wire rack to cool.

FOUGASSE

*450g/1lb/4 cups unbleached white
bread flour
5ml/1 tsp salt
20g/³⁄₄ oz fresh yeast
280ml/9fl oz/generous 1 cup
lukewarm water
15ml/1 tbsp extra virgin olive oil*

FOR THE FILLING
*50g/2oz/¹⁄₃ cup Roquefort
cheese, crumbled
40g/1¹⁄₂oz/¹⁄₃ cup walnut
pieces, chopped
25g/1oz/2 tbsp drained, canned
anchovy fillets, soaked in milk
and drained again, chopped
olive oil, for brushing*

MAKES 2 LOAVES

VARIATIONS
• Replace the cheese with 15ml/1 tbsp
chopped fresh sage or thyme or
40g/1½oz/⅓ cup chopped pitted olives.
• To make a sweet fougasse, replace
15ml/1 tbsp of the water with orange
flower water. Include 50g/2oz/⅓ cup
chopped candied orange peel and
25g/1oz/2 tbsp sugar.

*A fougasse is a lattice-shaped, flattish loaf from the South of France. It can be
cooked as a plain bread or flavoured with cheese, anchovies, herbs, nuts or
olives. On Christmas Eve in Provence a fougasse flavoured with orange
flower water is part of a table centrepiece of thirteen desserts, used to
symbolize Christ and the Twelve Apostles.*

1 Lightly grease two baking sheets. Sift
the flour and salt together into a large
bowl and make a well in the centre. In a
measuring jug (cup), cream the yeast
with 60ml/4 tbsp of the water. Pour the
yeast mixture into the centre of the
flour with the remaining water and the
olive oil and mix to a soft dough. Turn
out on to a lightly floured surface and
knead the dough for 8–10 minutes until
smooth and elastic.

2 Place the dough in a lightly oiled bowl,
cover with lightly oiled clear film (plastic
wrap) and leave in a warm place, for
about 1 hour, or until doubled in bulk.

3 Turn out on to a lightly floured surface
and knock back (punch down). Divide
into two equal pieces and flatten one
piece. Sprinkle over the cheese and
walnuts and fold the dough over on
itself two or three times to incorporate.
Repeat with the remaining piece of
dough using the anchovies. Shape each
piece of flavoured dough into a ball.

4 Flatten each ball of dough and fold the
bottom third up and the top third down,
to make an oblong. Roll the cheese
dough into a rectangle measuring about
28 × 15cm/11 × 6in. Using a sharp knife,
make four diagonal cuts almost to the
edge. Pull and stretch the dough evenly,
so that it resembles a ladder.

5 Shape the anchovy dough into an oval
with a flat base, about 25cm/10in long.
Using a sharp knife, make three diagonal
slits on each side towards the flat base,
and pull to open the cuts. Transfer to
the prepared baking sheets, cover with
lightly oiled clear film and leave to rise,
in a warm place, for about 30–45
minutes, or until nearly doubled in bulk.

6 Meanwhile, preheat the oven to 220°C/
425°F/Gas 7. Brush both loaves with a
little olive oil and bake for 25 minutes,
or until golden. Transfer to a wire rack
to cool.

CROISSANTS

350g/12oz/3 cups unbleached white
bread flour
115g/4oz/1 cup fine French plain
(all purpose) flour
5ml/1 tsp salt
25g/1oz/2 tbsp caster
(superfine) sugar
15g/½ oz fresh yeast
225ml/scant 8fl oz/scant 1 cup
lukewarm milk
1 egg, lightly beaten
225g/8oz/1 cup butter

FOR THE GLAZE
1 egg yolk
15ml/1 tbsp milk

MAKES 14 CROISSANTS

COOK'S TIP
Make sure that the block of butter
and the dough are about the same
temperature when combining, to
ensure the best results.

*Golden layers of flaky pastry, puffy, light and flavoured with butter, is how the
best croissants should be. Serve warm on the day of baking.*

3 Knock back (punch down), re-cover
and chill for 1 hour. Meanwhile, flatten
the butter into a block about 2cm/¾in
thick. Knock back the dough and turn
out on to a lightly floured surface. Roll
out into a rough 25cm/10in square,
rolling the edges thinner than the centre.

4 Place the block of butter diagonally in
the centre and fold the corners of the
dough over the butter like an envelope,
tucking in the edges to completely
enclose the butter.

1 Sift the flours and salt together into a
large bowl. Stir in the sugar. Make a well
in the centre. Cream the yeast with
45ml/3 tbsp of the milk, then stir in the
remainder. Add the yeast mixture to the
centre of the flour, then add the egg and
gradually beat in the flour until it forms
a dough.

2 Turn out on to a lightly floured surface
and knead for 3–4 minutes. Place in a
large lightly oiled bowl, cover with
lightly oiled clear (plastic wrap) film and
leave in a warm place, for about 45-60
minutes, or until doubled in bulk.

5 Roll the dough into a rectangle about
2cm/¾in thick, approximately twice as
long as it is wide. Fold the bottom third
up and the top third down and seal the
edges with a rolling pin. Wrap in clear
film and chill for 20 minutes.

6 Repeat the rolling, folding and chilling
twice more, turning the dough by
90 degrees each time. Roll out on a
floured surface into a 63 × 33cm/25 ×
13in rectangle; trim the edges to leave a
60 × 30cm/24 × 12in rectangle. Cut in
half lengthways. Cut crossways into
14 equal triangles with 15cm/6in bases.

7 Place the dough triangles on two
baking sheets, cover with clear film and
chill for 10 minutes.

8 To shape the croissants, place each
one with the wide end at the top, hold
each side and pull gently to stretch the
top of the triangle a little, then roll
towards the point, finishing with the
pointed end tucked underneath. Curve
the ends towards the pointed end to
make a crescent. Place on two baking
sheets, spaced well apart.

9 Mix together the egg yolk and milk
for the glaze. Lightly brush a little glaze
over the croissants, avoiding the cut
edges of the dough. Cover the croissants
loosely with lightly oiled clear film and
leave to rise, in a warm place, for about
30 minutes, or until they are nearly
doubled in size.

10 Meanwhile, preheat the oven to
220°C/425°F/Gas 7. Brush the croissants
with the remaining glaze and bake for
15–20 minutes, or until crisp and
golden. Transfer to a wire rack to cool
slightly before serving warm.

VARIATION
To make chocolate-filled croissants,
place a small square of milk or plain
(semisweet) chocolate or 15ml/1 tbsp
coarsely chopped chocolate at the
wide end of each triangle before
rolling up as in step 8.

FOR THE CHEF
50g/2oz/1/2 cup wholemeal
(whole-wheat) bread flour
45ml/3 tbsp warm water

FOR THE 1ST REFRESHMENT
60ml/4 tbsp warm water
75g/3oz/3/4 cup wholemeal bread flour

FOR THE 2ND REFRESHMENT
120ml/4fl oz/1/2 cup lukewarm water
115g/4oz/1 cup unbleached white
bread flour
25g/1oz/1/4 cup wholemeal bread flour

FOR THE DOUGH
150–175ml/5–6fl oz/2/3–3/4 cup
lukewarm water
350g/12oz/3 cups unbleached white
bread flour
10ml/2 tsp salt

MAKES 1 LOAF

COOK'S TIPS
• You will need to start making this bread about four days before you'd like to eat it.
• To make another loaf, keep the piece of starter dough (see step 6) in the refrigerator for up to three days. Use the reserved piece of starter dough for the 2nd refreshment in place of the *levain* in step 3, gradually mix in the water, then the flours and leave to rise as described.

1 To make the *chef*, place the flour in a small bowl, add the water and knead for 3–4 minutes to form a dough. Cover with clear film (plastic wrap) and leave the *chef* in a warm place for 2 days.

PAIN DE CAMPAGNE RUSTIQUE
——

This superb country bread is made using a natural French chef *starter to produce a rustic flavour and texture. In France, breads like this are often made three or four times the size of this loaf.*

2 Pull off the hardened crust and discard, then remove 30ml/2 tbsp of the moist centre. Place in a large bowl and gradually mix in the water for the 1st refreshment. Gradually mix in the flour and knead for 3–4 minutes to form a dough or *levain*, then cover with clear film and leave in a warm place for 1 day.

3 Discard the crust from the *levain* and gradually mix in the water for the 2nd refreshment. Mix in the flours a little at a time, mixing well after each addition to form a firm dough. Cover with lightly oiled clear film and leave to rise, in a warm place, for about 10 hours, or until doubled in bulk.

4 Lightly flour a baking sheet. For the final stage in the preparation of the dough, gradually mix the water into the *levain* in the bowl, then gradually mix in the flour, then the salt. Turn out the dough on to a lightly floured surface and knead for about 5 minutes until smooth and elastic.

5 Place the dough in a large lightly oiled bowl, cover with lightly oiled clear film and leave to rise, in a warm place, for 1½–2 hours, or until the dough has almost doubled in bulk.

6 Knock back (punch down) the dough and cut off 115g/4oz/½ cup. Set aside for making the next loaf. Shape the remaining dough into a ball – you should have about 350g/12oz/1½ cups.

7 Line a 10cm/4in high, 23cm/9in round basket or large bowl with a dishtowel and dust with flour.

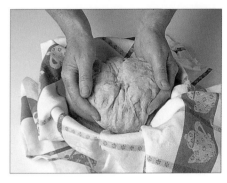

8 Place the dough ball seam side up in the prepared basket or bowl. Cover with lightly oiled clear film and leave to rise, in a warm place, for 2–3 hours, or until almost doubled in bulk.

9 Preheat the oven to 230°C/450°F/ Gas 8. Invert the loaf on to the prepared baking sheet and sprinkle with flour.

10 Slash the top of the loaf, using a sharp knife, four times at right angles to each other, to form a square pattern.

11 Sprinkle with a little more flour, if you like, then bake for 30–35 minutes, or until the loaf has browned and sounds hollow when tapped on the base. Transfer to a wire rack to cool.

BRIOCHE

—

Rich and buttery yet light and airy, this wonderful loaf captures the essence of the classic French bread.

1 Sift the flour and salt together into a large bowl and make a well in the centre. Put the yeast in a measuring jug (cup) and stir in the milk.

2 Add the yeast mixture to the centre of the flour with the eggs and mix together to form a soft dough.

3 Using your hand, beat the dough for 4–5 minutes until smooth and elastic. Cream the butter and sugar together. Gradually add the butter mixture to the dough in small amounts, making sure it is incorporated before adding more. Beat until smooth, shiny and elastic.

350g/12oz/3 cups unbleached white bread flour
2.5ml/$1/2$ tsp salt
15g/$1/2$ oz fresh yeast
60ml/4 tbsp lukewarm milk
3 eggs, lightly beaten
175g/6oz/$3/4$ cup butter, softened
25g/1oz/2 tbsp caster (superfine) sugar

FOR THE GLAZE
1 egg yolk
15ml/1 tbsp milk

MAKES 1 LOAF

4 Cover the bowl with lightly oiled clear film (plastic wrap) and leave the dough to rise, in a warm place, for 1–2 hours or until doubled in bulk.

5 Lightly knock back (punch down) the dough, then re-cover and place in the refrigerator for 8–10 hours or overnight.

6 Lightly grease a 1.6 litre/$2^3/4$ pint/ scant 7 cup brioche mould. Turn the dough out on to a lightly floured surface. Cut off almost a quarter and set aside. Shape the rest into a ball and place in the prepared mould. Shape the reserved dough into an elongated egg shape. Using two or three fingers, make a hole in the centre of the large ball of dough. Gently press the narrow end of the egg-shaped dough into the hole.

7 Mix together the egg yolk and milk for the glaze, and brush a little over the brioche. Cover with lightly oiled clear film and leave to rise, in a warm place, for 1$1/2$–2 hours, or until the dough nearly reaches the top of the mould.

8 Meanwhile, preheat the oven to 230°C/ 450°F/Gas 8. Brush the brioche with the remaining glaze and bake for 10 minutes. Reduce the oven temperature to 190°C/ 375°F/Gas 5 and bake for a further 20–25 minutes, or until golden. Turn out on to a wire rack to cool.

PAIN AUX NOIX

This delicious butter- and milk-enriched wholemeal bread is filled with walnuts. It is the perfect companion for cheese.

50g/2oz/¼ cup butter
350g/12oz/3 cups wholemeal (whole-wheat) bread flour
115g/4oz/1 cup unbleached white bread flour
15ml/1 tbsp light muscovado (brown) sugar
7.5ml/1½ tsp salt
20g/¾ oz fresh yeast
275ml/9fl oz/generous 1 cup lukewarm milk
175g/6oz/1½ cups walnut pieces

MAKES 2 LOAVES

3 Knead on a lightly floured surface for 6–8 minutes. Place in a lightly oiled bowl, cover with lightly oiled clear film (plastic wrap) and leave in a warm place, for 1 hour, or until doubled in bulk.

4 Turn out the dough on to a lightly floured surface and gently knock back (punch down). Press or roll out to flatten and then sprinkle over the nuts. Gently press the nuts into the dough, then roll it up. Return to the oiled bowl, re-cover and leave, in a warm place, for 30 minutes.

5 Turn out on to a lightly floured surface, divide in half and shape each piece into a ball. Place on the baking sheets, cover with lightly oiled clear film and leave to rise, in a warm place, for 45 minutes, or until doubled in bulk.

6 Meanwhile, preheat the oven to 220°C/425°F/Gas 7. Using a sharp knife, slash the top of each loaf three times. Bake for about 35 minutes, or until the loaves sound hollow when tapped on the base. Transfer to a wire rack to cool.

1 Lightly grease two baking sheets. Place the butter in a small pan and heat until melted and starting to turn brown, then set aside to cool. Mix the flours, sugar and salt in a large bowl and make a well in the centre. Cream the yeast with half the milk. Add to the centre of the flour with the remaining milk.

2 Pour the cool melted butter through a fine strainer into the centre of the flour so that it joins the liquids already there. Using your hand, mix the liquids together in the bowl and gradually mix in small quantities of the flour to make a batter. Continue until the mixture forms a moist dough.

*450g/1lb/4 cups unbleached white
bread flour
10ml/2 tsp salt
15ml/1 tbsp caster (superfine) sugar
50g/2oz/1/4 cup butter, softened
15g/1/2 oz fresh yeast
280ml/9fl oz/generous 1 cup
lukewarm milk, plus 15ml/1 tbsp
extra milk, for glazing*

MAKES 12 ROLLS

*400g/14oz/3 1/2 cups unbleached white
bread flour
7.5ml/1 1/2 tsp salt
5ml/1 tsp caster (superfine) sugar
15g/1/2 oz fresh yeast
120ml/4fl oz/1/2 cup lukewarm milk
175ml/6fl oz/3/4 cup lukewarm water*

MAKES 10 ROLLS

1 Grease two baking sheets. Sift the
flour and salt into a large bowl. Stir in
the sugar and make a well in the centre.

2 Cream the yeast with the milk until
dissolved, then pour into the centre of
the flour mixture. Sprinkle over a little
of the flour from around the edge. Leave
at room temperature for 15–20 minutes,
or until the mixture starts to bubble.

PETITS PAINS AU LAIT

*These classic French round milk rolls have a soft crust and a light, slightly
sweet crumb. They won't last long!*

1 Lightly grease two baking sheets. Sift
the flour and salt together into a large
bowl. Stir in the sugar. Rub the softened
butter into the flour.

2 Cream the yeast with 60ml/4 tbsp of the
milk. Stir in the remaining milk. Pour into
the flour mixture and mix to a soft dough.

3 Turn out on to a lightly floured surface
and knead for 8–10 minutes until
smooth and elastic. Place in a lightly
oiled bowl, cover with lightly oiled clear
film (plastic wrap) and leave in a warm
place, for 1 hour, or until doubled in bulk.

4 Turn out the dough on to a lightly
floured surface and gently knock back
(punch down). Divide into 12 equal
pieces. Shape into balls and space on
the baking sheets.

5 Using a sharp knife, cut a cross in the
top of each roll. Cover with lightly oiled
clear film and leave to rise, in a warm
place, for about 20 minutes, or until
doubled in size.

6 Preheat the oven to 200°C/400°F/
Gas 6. Brush the rolls with milk and
bake for 20–25 minutes, or until golden.
Transfer to a wire rack to cool.

FRENCH DIMPLED ROLLS

*A French and Belgian speciality, these attractive rolls are distinguished by
the split down the centre. They have a crusty finish while remaining soft and
light inside – they taste lovely, too.*

3 Add the water and gradually mix in
the flour to form a fairly moist, soft
dough. Turn out on to a lightly floured
surface and knead for 8–10 minutes
until smooth and elastic. Place in a
lightly oiled bowl, cover with lightly
oiled clear film (plastic wrap) and leave
to rise, at room temperature, for about
1 1/2 hours, or until doubled in bulk.

4 Turn out on to a lightly floured surface
and knock back (punch down). Re-cover
and leave to rest for 5 minutes. Divide
into 10 pieces. Shape into balls by
rolling the dough under a cupped hand,
then roll until oval. Lightly flour the tops.
Space well apart on the baking sheets,
cover with lightly oiled clear film and
leave at room temperature, for about 30
minutes, or until almost doubled in size.

5 Lightly oil the side of your hand and
press the centre of each roll to make a
deep split. Re-cover and leave to rest for
15 minutes. Meanwhile, place a roasting
pan in the bottom of the oven and
preheat the oven to 230°C/450°F/Gas 8.
Pour 250ml/8fl oz/1 cup water into the
tin and bake the rolls for 15 minutes, or
until golden. Cool on a wire rack.

PUGLIESE

This classic Italian open-textured, soft-crumbed bread is moistened and flavoured with fruity olive oil. Its floured top gives it a true country feel.

FOR THE BIGA STARTER
175g/6oz/1¹/₂ cups unbleached white bread flour
7g/¹/₄ oz fresh yeast
90ml/6 tbsp lukewarm water

FOR THE DOUGH
225g/8oz/2 cups unbleached white bread flour, plus extra for dusting
225g/8oz/2 cups unbleached wholemeal (whole-wheat) bread flour
5ml/1 tsp caster (superfine) sugar
10ml/2 tsp salt
15g/¹/₂ oz fresh yeast
275ml/9fl oz/generous 1 cup lukewarm water
75ml/5 tbsp extra virgin olive oil

MAKES 1 LARGE LOAF

VARIATION
Incorporate 150g/5oz/1 cup chopped black olives into the dough at the end of step 5 for extra olive flavour.

1 Sift the flour for the *biga* starter into a large bowl. Make a well in the centre. In a small bowl, cream the yeast with the water. Pour the liquid into the centre of the flour and gradually mix in the surrounding flour to form a firm dough.

2 Turn the dough out on to a lightly floured surface and knead for 5 minutes until smooth and elastic. Return to the bowl, cover with lightly oiled clear film (plastic wrap) and leave to rise, in a warm place, for 8–10 hours, or until the dough has risen well and is starting to collapse.

3 Lightly flour a baking sheet. Mix the flours, sugar and salt for the dough in a large bowl. Cream the yeast and the water in another large bowl, then stir in the *biga* and mix together.

4 Stir in the flour mixture a little at a time, then add the olive oil in the same way, and mix to a soft dough. Turn out on to a lightly floured surface and knead the dough for 8–10 minutes until smooth and elastic.

5 Place in a lightly oiled bowl, cover with lightly oiled clear film and leave to rise, in a warm place, for 1–1¹/₂ hours, or until doubled in bulk.

6 Turn out on to a lightly floured surface and knock back (punch down). Gently pull out the edges and fold under to make a round. Transfer to the prepared baking sheet, cover with lightly oiled clear film and leave to rise, in a warm place, for 1–1¹/₂ hours, or until almost doubled in size.

7 Meanwhile, preheat the oven to 230°C/450°F/Gas 8. Lightly dust the loaf with flour and bake for 15 minutes. Reduce the oven temperature to 200°C/400°F/Gas 6 and bake for a further 20 minutes, or until the loaf sounds hollow when tapped on the base. Transfer to a wire rack to cool.

CIABATTA

This irregular-shaped Italian bread is so called because it looks like an old shoe or slipper. It is made with a very wet dough flavoured with olive oil; cooking produces a bread with holes and a wonderfully chewy crust.

1 Cream the yeast for the *biga* starter with a little of the water. Sift the flour into a large bowl. Gradually mix in the yeast mixture and sufficient of the remaining water to form a firm dough.

2 Turn out the *biga* starter dough on to a lightly floured surface and knead for about 5 minutes until smooth and elastic. Return the dough to the bowl, cover with lightly oiled clear film (plastic wrap) and leave in a warm place for 12–15 hours, or until the dough has risen and is starting to collapse.

3 Sprinkle three baking sheets with flour. Mix the yeast for the dough with a little of the water until creamy, then mix in the remainder. Add the yeast mixture to the *biga* and gradually mix in.

4 Mix in the milk, beating thoroughly with a wooden spoon. Using your hand, gradually beat in the flour, lifting the dough as you mix. Mixing the dough will take 15 minutes or more and form a very wet mix, impossible to knead on a work surface.

5 Beat in the salt and olive oil. Cover with lightly oiled clear film and leave to rise, in a warm place, for 1½–2 hours, or until doubled in bulk.

6 With a spoon, carefully tip one-third of the dough at a time on to the baking sheets without knocking back (punching down) the dough in the process.

7 Using floured hands, shape into rough oblong loaf shapes, about 2.5cm/1in thick. Flatten slightly with splayed fingers. Sprinkle with flour and leave to rise in a warm place for 30 minutes.

8 Meanwhile, preheat the oven to 220°C/425°F/Gas 7. Bake for 25–30 minutes, or until golden brown and sounding hollow when tapped on the base. Transfer to a wire rack to cool.

FOR THE BIGA STARTER
7g/¼ oz fresh yeast
175–200ml/6–7fl oz/¾–scant 1 cup lukewarm water
350g/12oz/3 cups unbleached plain (all-purpose) flour, plus extra for dusting

FOR THE DOUGH
15g/½ oz fresh yeast
400ml/14fl oz/1⅔ cups lukewarm water
60ml/4 tbsp lukewarm milk
500g/1¼ lb/5 cups unbleached white bread flour
10ml/2 tsp salt
45ml/3 tbsp extra virgin olive oil

MAKES 3 LOAVES

VARIATION
To make tomato-flavoured ciabatta, add 115g/4oz/1 cup chopped, drained sun-dried tomatoes in olive oil. Add with the olive oil in step 5.

OLIVE BREAD

Black and green olives and good-quality fruity olive oil combine to make this strongly flavoured and irresistible Italian bread.

1 Lightly grease a baking sheet. Mix the flours, yeast and salt together in a large bowl and make a well in the centre.

2 Add the water and oil to the centre of the flour and mix to a soft dough. Knead the dough on a lightly floured surface for 8–10 minutes until smooth and elastic. Place in a lightly oiled bowl, cover with lightly oiled clear film (plastic wrap) and leave in a warm place, for 1 hour, or until doubled in bulk.

3 Turn out on to a lightly floured surface and knock back (punch down). Flatten out and sprinkle over the olives. Fold up and knead to distribute the olives. Leave to rest for 5 minutes, then shape into an oval loaf. Place on the baking sheet.

4 Make six deep cuts in the top of the loaf, and gently push the sections over. Cover with lightly oiled clear film and leave to rise, in a warm place, for 30–45 minutes, or until doubled in size.

275g/10oz/2¹/₂ cups unbleached white bread flour
50g/2oz/¹/₂ cup wholemeal (whole-wheat) bread flour
6g/¹/₄ oz sachet easy-blend (rapid-rise) dried yeast
2.5ml/¹/₂ tsp salt
210ml/7¹/₂ fl oz/ 1 cup lukewarm water
15ml/1 tbsp extra virgin olive oil, plus extra, for brushing
115g/4oz/1 cup pitted black and green olives, coarsely chopped

MAKES 1 LOAF

VARIATIONS
• Increase the proportion of wholemeal flour to make the loaf more rustic.
• Add some hazelnuts or pine nuts.

5 Meanwhile, preheat the oven to 200°C/ 400°F/Gas 6. Brush the bread with olive oil and bake for 35 minutes. Transfer to a wire rack to cool.

PANINI ALL'OLIO

450g/1lb/4 cups unbleached white bread flour
10ml/2 tsp salt
15g/¹/₂ oz fresh yeast
250ml/8fl oz/1 cup lukewarm water
60ml/4 tbsp extra virgin olive oil, plus extra for brushing

MAKES 16 ROLLS

The Italians adore interesting and elaborately shaped rolls. This distinctively flavoured bread dough, enriched with olive oil, can be used for making rolls or shaped as one large loaf.

1 Lightly oil three baking sheets. Sift the flour and salt together in a large bowl and make a well in the centre.

2 In a jug (pitcher), cream the yeast with half of the water, then stir in the remainder. Add to the centre of the flour with the oil and mix to a dough.

3 Turn the dough out on to a lightly floured surface and knead for 8–10 minutes until smooth and elastic. Place in a lightly oiled bowl, cover with lightly oiled clear film (plastic wrap) and leave in a warm place, for about 1 hour, or until nearly doubled in bulk.

4 Turn on to a lightly floured surface and knock back (punch down). Divide into 12 equal pieces of dough and shape into rolls as described in steps 5, 6 and 7.

5 For *tavalli* (twisted spiral rolls): roll each piece of dough into a strip about 30cm/12in long and 4cm/1½ in wide. Twist each strip into a loose spiral and join the ends of dough together to make a circle. Place on the prepared baking sheets, spaced well apart. Brush the *tavalli* lightly with olive oil, cover with lightly oiled clear film and leave to rise, in a warm place, for 20–30 minutes.

6 For *filoncini* (finger-shaped rolls): flatten each piece of dough into an oval and roll to about 23cm/9in in length without changing the basic shape. Make it 5cm/2in wide at one end and 10cm/4in wide at the other. Roll up, starting from the wider end. Using your fingers, gently stretch the dough roll to 20–23cm/8–9in long. Cut in half. Place on the prepared baking sheets, spaced well apart. Brush the finger shapes with olive oil, cover with lightly oiled clear film and leave to rise, in a warm place, for 20–30 minutes.

7 For *carciofi* (artichoke-shaped rolls): shape each piece of dough into a ball and space well apart on the prepared baking sheets. Brush with olive oil, cover with lightly oiled clear film and leave to rise, in a warm place, for 20–30 minutes. Meanwhile, preheat the oven to 200°C/400°F/Gas 6. Using scissors, snip four or five 5mm/¼ in deep cuts in a circle on the top of each *carciofo*, then make five larger horizontal cuts around the sides. Bake the rolls for 15 minutes. Transfer to a wire rack to cool.

FOCACCIA

This simple dimple-topped Italian flat bread is punctuated with olive oil and the aromatic flavours of sage and garlic to produce a truly succulent loaf.

20g/¾ oz fresh yeast
325–350ml/11–12fl oz/1⅓–1½ cups lukewarm water
45ml/3 tbsp extra virgin olive oil
500g/1¼ lb/5 cups unbleached white bread flour
10ml/2 tsp salt
15ml/1 tbsp chopped fresh sage

FOR THE TOPPING
60ml/4 tbsp extra virgin olive oil
4 garlic cloves, chopped
12 fresh sage leaves

MAKES 2 ROUND LOAVES

VARIATION
Flavour the bread with other herbs, such as oregano, basil or rosemary and top with chopped black olives.

4 Knock back (punch down) and turn out on to a lightly floured surface. Gently knead in the chopped sage. Divide the dough into two equal pieces. Shape each into a ball, roll out into 25cm/10in circles and place in the prepared tins.

1 Lightly oil 2 × 25cm/10in shallow round cake tins (pans) or pizza pans. Cream the yeast with 60ml/4 tbsp of the water, then stir in the remaining water. Stir in the oil.

2 Sift the flour and salt together into a large bowl and make a well in the centre. Pour the yeast mixture into the well in the centre of the flour and mix to a soft dough.

3 Turn out the dough on to a lightly floured surface and knead for 8–10 minutes until smooth and elastic. Place in a lightly oiled bowl, cover with lightly oiled clear film (plastic wrap) or a large, lightly oiled plastic bag, and leave to rise, in a warm place, for about 1–1½ hours, or until doubled in bulk.

5 Cover with lightly oiled clear film and leave to rise in a warm place for about 30 minutes. Uncover, and using your fingertips, poke the dough to make deep dimples over the entire surface. Replace the clear film cover and leave to rise until doubled in bulk.

6 Meanwhile, preheat the oven to 200°C/400°F/Gas 6. Drizzle over the olive oil for the topping and sprinkle each focaccia evenly with chopped garlic. Dot the sage leaves over the surface. Bake for 25–30 minutes, or until both loaves are golden. Immediately remove the focaccia from the tins and transfer them to a wire rack to cool slightly. These loaves are best served warm.

PANE TOSCANO

—

This bread from Tuscany is made without salt and probably originates from the days when salt was heavily taxed. To compensate for the lack of salt, this bread is usually served with salty foods, such as anchovies and olives.

550g/1¼ lb/5 cups unbleached white bread flour
350ml/12fl oz/1½ cups boiling water
15g/½ oz fresh yeast
60ml/4 tbsp lukewarm water

MAKES 1 LOAF

1 First make the starter. Sift 175g/6oz/ 1½ cups of the flour into a large bowl. Pour over the boiling water, leave for a couple of minutes, then mix well. Cover the bowl with a damp dishtowel and leave for 10 hours.

2 Lightly flour a baking sheet. Cream the yeast with the lukewarm water. Stir into the starter.

3 Gradually add the remaining flour and mix to form a dough. Turn out on to a lightly floured surface and knead for 5–8 minutes until smooth and elastic.

4 Place in a lightly oiled bowl, cover with lightly oiled clear film (plastic wrap) and leave in a warm place, for 1–1½ hours, or until doubled in bulk.

5 Turn out the dough on to a lightly floured surface, knock back (punch down), and shape into a round.

COOK'S TIP
Salt controls the action of yeast in bread so the leavening action is more noticeable. Don't let this unsalted bread over-rise or it may collapse.

6 Fold the sides of the round into the centre and seal. Place seam side up on the prepared baking sheet. Cover with lightly oiled clear film and leave to rise, in a warm place, for 30–45 minutes, or until doubled in size.

7 Flatten the loaf to about half its risen height and flip over. Cover with a large upturned bowl and leave to rise, in a warm place, for 30 minutes.

8 Meanwhile, preheat the oven to 220°C/ 425°F/Gas 7. Slash the top of the loaf, using a sharp knife, if wished. Bake for 30–35 minutes, or until golden. Transfer to a wire rack to cool.

SICILIAN SCROLL

A wonderful pale yellow, crusty-topped loaf, enhanced with a nutty flavour from the sesame seeds. It's perfect for serving with cheese.

450g/1lb/4 cups finely ground
semolina
115g/4oz/1 cup unbleached white
bread flour
10ml/2 tsp salt
20g/³/4 oz fresh yeast
360ml/12¹/2 fl oz/generous 1¹/2 cups
lukewarm water
30ml/2 tbsp extra virgin olive oil
sesame seeds, for sprinkling

MAKES 1 LOAF

1 Lightly grease a baking sheet. Mix the semolina, white bread flour and salt together in a large bowl and make a well in the centre.

2 In a jug (pitcher), cream the yeast with half the water, then stir in the remainder. Add the creamed yeast to the centre of the semolina mixture with the olive oil and gradually incorporate the semolina and flour to form a firm dough.

3 Turn out the dough on to a lightly floured surface and knead for 8–10 minutes until smooth and elastic. Place in a lightly oiled bowl, cover with lightly oiled clear film (plastic wrap) and leave to rise, in a warm place, for 1–1¹/2 hours, or until the dough has doubled in bulk.

4 Turn out on to a lightly floured surface and knock back (punch down). Knead gently, then shape into a fat roll about 50cm/20in long. Form into an "S" shape.

5 Carefully transfer the dough to the prepared baking sheet, cover with lightly oiled clear film and leave to rise, in a warm place, for 30–45 minutes, or until doubled in size.

6 Meanwhile, preheat the oven to 220°C/ 425°F/Gas 7. Brush the top of the scroll with water and sprinkle with sesame seeds. Bake for 10 minutes. Spray the inside of the oven with water twice during this time. Reduce the oven temperature to 200°C/400°F/Gas 6 and bake for a further 25–30 minutes, or until golden. Transfer to a wire rack to cool.

VARIATION
Although sesame seeds are the traditional topping on this delectable Italian bread, poppy seeds, or even crystals of sea salt, could be used instead.

*225g/8oz/2 cups unbleached white
bread flour
7.5ml/1½ tsp salt
15g/½ oz fresh yeast
135ml/4½ fl oz/scant ⅔ cup lukewarm
water
30ml/2 tbsp extra virgin olive oil,
plus extra for brushing
sesame seeds, for coating*

MAKES 20 GRISSINI

*175g/6oz/1½ cups unbleached
white flour
5ml/1 tsp salt
15ml/1 tbsp olive oil
105ml/7 tbsp lukewarm water*

MAKES 4 PIADINE

SESAME-STUDDED GRISSINI

—

*These crisp, pencil-like breadsticks are easy to make and far more delicious
than the commercially manufactured grissini. Once you start to nibble one, it
will be difficult to stop.*

1 Lightly oil two baking sheets. Sift the
flour and salt together into a large bowl
and make a well in the centre.

2 In a jug (pitcher), cream the yeast
with the water. Pour into the centre
of the flour, add the olive oil and mix
to a soft dough. Turn out on to a lightly
floured surface and knead for
8–10 minutes until smooth and elastic.

3 Roll the dough into a rectangle about
15 × 20cm/6 × 8in. Brush with olive oil,
cover with lightly oiled clear film
(plastic wrap) and leave in a warm place,
for about 1 hour, or until doubled in bulk.

4 Preheat the oven to 200°C/400°F/
Gas 6. Spread out the sesame seeds.
Cut the dough in two 7.5 x 10cm/3 x 4in
rectangles. Cut each piece into ten
7.5cm/3in strips. Stretch each strip
gently until it is about 30cm/12in long.

5 Roll each grissini, as it is made, in the
sesame seeds. Place the grissini on the
prepared baking sheets, spaced well
apart. Lightly brush with olive oil. Leave
to rise, in a warm place, for 10 minutes,
then bake for 15–20 minutes. Transfer
to a wire rack to cool.

PIADINE

—

*These soft unleavened Italian breads, cooked directly on the hob, were
originally cooked on a hot stone over an open fire. They are best eaten while
still warm. Try them as an accompaniment to soups and dips.*

1 Sift the flour and salt together into a
large bowl; make a well in the centre.

2 Add the oil and water to the centre of
the flour and gradually mix in to form a
dough. Knead on a lightly floured
surface for 4–5 minutes until smooth
and elastic. Place in a lightly oiled bowl,
cover with oiled clear film (plastic wrap)
and leave to rest for 20 minutes.

3 Heat a griddle over a medium heat.
Divide the dough into four equal pieces
and roll each into an 18cm/7in round.
Cover until ready to cook.

4 Lightly oil the hot griddle, add one or
two piadine and cook for about 2
minutes, or until they are starting to
brown. Turn the piadine over and cook
for a further 1–1½ minutes. Serve warm.

PANETTONE

This classic Italian bread can be found throughout Italy around Christmas. It is a surprisingly light bread even though it is rich with butter and dried fruit.

400g/14oz/3½ cups unbleached white bread flour
2.5ml/½ tsp salt
15g/½ oz fresh yeast
120ml/4fl oz/½ cup lukewarm milk
2 eggs plus 2 egg yolks
75g/3oz/6 tbsp caster (superfine) sugar
150g/5oz/⅔ cup butter, softened
115g/4oz/⅔ cup mixed chopped (candied) peel
75g/3oz/½ cup raisins
melted butter, for brushing

MAKES 1 LOAF

COOK'S TIP
Once the dough has been enriched with butter, do not prove in too warm a place or the loaf will become greasy.

1 Using a double layer of baking parchment, line and butter a 15cm/6in deep cake tin (pan) or soufflé dish. Finish the paper 7.5cm/3in above the top of the tin.

2 Sift the flour and salt together into a large bowl. Make a well in the centre. Cream the yeast with 60ml/4 tbsp of the milk, then mix in the remainder.

3 Pour the yeast mixture into the centre of the flour, add the whole eggs and mix in sufficient flour to make a thick batter. Sprinkle a little of the remaining flour over the top and leave to "sponge", in a warm place, for 30 minutes.

4 Add the egg yolks and sugar and mix to a soft dough. Work in the softened butter, then turn out on to a lightly floured surface and knead for 5 minutes until smooth and elastic. Place in a lightly oiled bowl, cover with lightly oiled clear film (plastic wrap) and leave to rise, in a slightly warm place, for 1½–2 hours, or until doubled in bulk.

5 Knock back (punch down) the dough and turn out on to a lightly floured surface. Gently knead in the peel and raisins. Shape into a ball and place in the prepared tin. Cover with lightly oiled clear film and leave to rise, in a slightly warm place, for about 1 hour, or until doubled.

6 Meanwhile, preheat the oven to 190°C/375°F/Gas 5. Brush the surface with melted butter and cut a cross in the top using a sharp knife. Bake for 20 minutes, then reduce the oven temperature to 180°C/350°F/Gas 4. Brush the top with butter again and bake for a further 25–30 minutes, or until golden. Cool in the tin for 5–10 minutes, then turn out on to a wire rack to cool.

SCHIACCIATA

This Tuscan version of Italian pizza-style flat bread can be rolled to varying thicknesses to give either a crisp or soft, bread-like finish.

350g/12oz/3 cups unbleached white bread flour
2.5ml/½ tsp salt
15g/½ oz fresh yeast
200ml/7fl oz/scant 1 cup lukewarm water
60ml/4 tbsp extra virgin olive oil

FOR THE TOPPING
30ml/2 tbsp extra virgin olive oil, for brushing
30ml/2 tbsp fresh rosemary leaves
coarse sea salt, for sprinkling

MAKES 1 LARGE LOAF

1 Lightly oil a baking sheet. Sift the flour and salt into a large bowl and make a well in the centre. Cream the yeast with half the water. Add to the centre of the flour with the remaining water and olive oil and mix to a soft dough. Turn out the dough on to a lightly floured surface and knead for 10 minutes until smooth and elastic.

2 Place in a lightly oiled bowl, cover with lightly oiled clear film (plastic wrap) and leave to rise, in a warm place, for about 1 hour, or until doubled in bulk.

3 Knock back (punch down) the dough, turn out on to a lightly floured surface and knead gently. Roll to a 30 × 20cm/ 12 × 8in rectangle and place on the prepared baking sheet. Brush with some of the olive oil for the topping and cover with lightly oiled clear film.

4 Leave to rise, in a warm place, for about 20 minutes, then brush with the remaining oil, prick all over with a fork and sprinkle with rosemary and sea salt. Leave to rise again in a warm place for 15 minutes.

5 Meanwhile, preheat the oven to 200°C/ 400°F/Gas 6. Bake for 30 minutes, or until light golden. Transfer to a wire rack to cool slightly. Serve warm.

PITTA BREAD

These Turkish breads are a firm favourite in both the eastern Mediterranean and the Middle East, and have crossed to England and the USA. This versatile soft, flat bread forms a pocket as it cooks, which is perfect for filling with vegetables, salads or meats.

225g/8oz/2 cups unbleached white
bread flour
5ml/1 tsp salt
15g/1/2 oz fresh yeast
140ml/scant 1/4 pint/scant 2/3 cup
lukewarm water
10ml/2 tsp extra virgin olive oil

MAKES 6 PITTA BREADS

VARIATIONS
To make wholemeal (whole-wheat) pitta breads, replace half the white bread flour with wholemeal bread flour. You can also make smaller round pitta breads about 10cm/4in in diameter to serve as snack breads.

5 Roll out each ball of dough in turn to an oval about 5mm/1/4in thick and 15cm/6in long. Place on a floured dishtowel and cover with lightly oiled clear film. Leave to rise at room temperature for about 20–30 minutes.

1 Sift the flour and salt together into a bowl. Mix the yeast with the water until dissolved, then stir in the olive oil and pour into a large bowl.

2 Gradually beat the flour into the yeast mixture, then knead the mixture to make a soft dough.

3 Turn out on to a lightly floured surface and knead for 5 minutes until smooth and elastic. Place in a large bowl, cover with lightly oiled clear film (plastic wrap) and leave to rise, in a warm place, for 1 hour, or until doubled in bulk.

4 Knock back (punch down) the dough. On a floured surface, divide into six equal pieces and shape into balls. Cover with oiled clear film; rest for 5 minutes.

6 Meanwhile, preheat the oven to 230°C/ 450°F/Gas 8. Place three baking sheets in the oven to heat at the same time.

7 Place two pitta breads on each baking sheet and bake for 4–6 minutes, or until puffed up; they do not need to brown. If preferred, cook the pitta bread in batches. It is important that the oven has reached the recommended temperature before the pitta breads are baked. This ensures that they puff up.

8 Transfer the pittas to a wire rack to cool until warm, then cover with a dishtowel to keep them soft.

PAN DE CEBADA

This Spanish country bread has a close, heavy texture and is quite satisfying.
It is richly flavoured, incorporating barley and maize flours.

FOR THE SOURDOUGH STARTER
175g/6oz/1½ cups corn meal
560ml/scant 1 pint/scant 2½ cups
water
225g/8oz/2 cups wholemeal
(whole-wheat) bread flour
75g/3oz/¾ cup barley flour

FOR THE DOUGH
20g/¾ oz fresh yeast
45ml/3 tbsp lukewarm water
225g/8oz/2 cups wholemeal
bread flour
15ml/1 tbsp salt
corn meal, for dusting

MAKES 1 LARGE LOAF

1 In a pan, mix the corn meal for the sourdough starter with half the water, then blend in the remainder. Cook over a gentle heat, stirring continuously, until thickened. Transfer to a large bowl and set aside to cool.

2 Mix in the wholemeal flour and barley flour. Turn out on to a lightly floured surface and knead for 5 minutes. Return to the bowl, cover with lightly oiled clear film (plastic wrap) and leave the starter in a warm place for 36 hours.

5 Knock back (punch down) the dough and turn out on to a lightly floured surface. Shape into a plump round. Sprinkle with a little corn meal.

6 Place the shaped bread on the prepared baking sheet. Cover with a large upturned bowl. Leave to rise, in a warm place, for about 1 hour, or until nearly doubled in bulk. Place an empty roasting pan in the bottom of the oven. Preheat the oven to 220°C/425°F/Gas 7.

7 Pour 300ml/½ pint/1¼ cups cold water into the roasting pan. Lift the bowl off the risen loaf and immediately place the baking sheet in the oven. Bake the bread for 10 minutes. Remove the pan of water, reduce the oven temperature to 190°C/375°F/Gas 5 and bake for about 20 minutes. Cool on a wire rack.

3 Dust a baking sheet with corn meal. In a small bowl, cream the yeast with the water for the dough. Mix the yeast mixture into the starter with the wholemeal flour and salt and work to a dough. Turn out on to a lightly floured surface and knead for 4–5 minutes until smooth and elastic.

4 Transfer the dough to a lightly oiled bowl, cover with lightly oiled clear film or an oiled plastic bag and leave, in a warm place, for 1½–2 hours to rise, or until nearly doubled in bulk.

MALLORCAN ENSAIMADAS

These spiral- or snail-shaped rolls are a popular Spanish breakfast treat. Traditionally lard or saim *was used to brush over the strips of sweetened dough, but nowadays mainly butter is used to add a delicious richness.*

225g/8oz/2 cups unbleached white bread flour
2.5ml/½ tsp salt
50g/2oz/¼ cup caster (superfine) sugar
15g/½ oz fresh yeast
75ml/5 tbsp lukewarm milk
1 egg
30ml/2 tbsp sunflower oil
50g/2oz/¼ cup butter, melted
icing (confectioners') sugar, for dusting

MAKES 16 ROLLS

1 Lightly grease two baking sheets. Sift the flour and salt together into a large mixing bowl. Stir in the sugar and make a well in the centre.

2 Cream the yeast with the milk, pour into the centre of the flour mixture, then sprinkle a little of the flour mixture evenly over the top of the liquid. Leave in a warm place for about 15 minutes, or until frothy.

3 In a small bowl, beat the egg and sunflower oil together. Add to the flour mixture and mix to a smooth dough.

4 Turn out on to a lightly floured surface and knead for 8–10 minutes until smooth and elastic. Place in a lightly oiled bowl, cover with lightly oiled clear film (plastic wrap) and leave in a warm place, for 1 hour, or until doubled in bulk.

5 Turn out the dough on to a lightly floured surface. Knock back (punch down) and divide the dough into 16 equal pieces. Shape each piece into a thin rope about 38cm/15in long. Pour the melted butter on to a plate and dip the ropes into the butter to coat.

6 On the baking sheets, curl each rope into a loose spiral, spacing well apart. Tuck the ends under to seal. Cover with lightly oiled clear film and leave to rise, in a warm place, for about 45 minutes, or until doubled in size.

7 Meanwhile, preheat the oven to 190°C/375°F/Gas 5. Brush the rolls with water and dust with icing sugar. Bake for 10 minutes, or until light golden brown. Cool on a wire rack. Dust again with icing sugar and serve warm.

GREEK OLIVE BREAD

675g/1¹/₂ lb/6 cups unbleached white
bread flour, plus extra
for dusting
10ml/2 tsp salt
25g/1oz fresh yeast
350ml/12fl oz/1¹/₂ cups lukewarm
water
75ml/5 tbsp olive oil
175g/6oz/1¹/₂ cups pitted black olives,
roughly chopped
1 red onion, finely chopped
30ml/2 tbsp chopped fresh coriander
(cilantro) or mint

MAKES 2 LOAVES

VARIATION
Make one large loaf and increase the
baking time by about 15 minutes.

*The flavours of the Mediterranean simply ooze from this decorative bread,
speckled with black olives, red onions and herbs.*

1 Lightly grease two baking sheets. Sift
the flour and salt together into a large
bowl and make a well in the centre.

2 In a jug (pitcher), blend the yeast
with half of the water. Add to the centre
of the flour with the remaining water
and the olive oil; mix to a soft dough.

3 Turn out the dough on to a lightly
floured surface and knead for 8–10
minutes until smooth. Place in a lightly
oiled bowl, cover with lightly oiled clear
film (plastic wrap) and leave to rise, in a
warm place, for 1 hour, or until doubled
in bulk.

4 Turn out on to a lightly floured surface
and knock back (punch down). Cut off a
quarter of the dough, cover with lightly
oiled clear film and set aside.

5 Roll out the remaining, large piece of
dough to a round. Sprinkle the olives,
onion and herbs evenly over the surface,
then bring up the sides of the circle and
gently knead together. Cut the dough in
half and shape each piece into a plump
oval loaf, about 20cm/8in long. Place on
the prepared baking sheets.

6 Divide the reserved dough into
four equal pieces and roll each to a long
strand 60cm/24in long. Twist together
and cut in half. Brush the centre of each
loaf with water and place two pieces of
twisted dough on top of each, tucking
the ends underneath the loaves.

7 Cover with lightly oiled clear film and
leave to rise, in a warm place, for about
45 minutes, or until the loaves are
plump and nearly doubled in size.

8 Meanwhile, preheat the oven to 220°C/
425°F/Gas 7. Dust the loaves lightly with
flour and bake for 35–40 minutes, or
until golden and sounding hollow when
tapped on the base. Transfer to a wire
rack to cool.

MOROCCAN HOLIDAY BREAD

The addition of corn meal and a cornucopia of seeds gives this superb loaf an interesting flavour and texture.

275g/10oz/2¹/2 cups unbleached white bread flour
50g/2oz/¹/2 cup cornmeal
5ml/1 tsp salt
20g/³/4 oz fresh yeast
120ml/4fl oz/¹/2 cup lukewarm water
120ml/4fl oz/¹/2 cup lukewarm milk
15ml/1 tbsp pumpkin seeds
15ml/1 tbsp sesame seeds
30ml/2 tbsp sunflower seeds

MAKES 1 LOAF

5 Turn out the dough on to a lightly floured surface and knock back (punch down). Gently knead the pumpkin and sesame seeds into the dough. Shape into a round ball and flatten slightly.

6 Place on the prepared baking sheet, cover with lightly oiled clear film or slide into a large, lightly oiled plastic bag and leave to rise, in a warm place, for 45 minutes, or until doubled in bulk.

1 Lightly grease a baking sheet. Sift the flours and salt into a large bowl.

2 Cream the yeast with a little of the water in a jug (pitcher). Stir in the remainder of the water and the milk. Pour into the centre of the flour and mix to a fairly soft dough.

3 Turn out the dough on to a lightly floured surface and knead for about 5 minutes until smooth and elastic.

4 Place in a lightly oiled bowl, cover with lightly oiled clear film (plastic wrap) and leave in a warm place, for about 1 hour, or until doubled in bulk.

VARIATIONS
Incorporate all the seeds in the dough in step 5 and leave the top of the loaf plain. Alternatively, use sesame seeds instead of sunflower seeds for the topping and either incorporate the sunflower seeds in the loaf or leave them out.

7 Meanwhile, preheat the oven to 200°C/400°F/Gas 6. Brush the top of the loaf with water and sprinkle evenly with the sunflower seeds. Bake the loaf for 30–35 minutes, or until it is golden and sounds hollow when tapped on the base. Transfer the loaf to a wire rack to cool.

SWISS BRAID

350g/12oz/3 cups unbleached white
bread flour
5ml/1 tsp salt
20g/¾ oz fresh yeast
30ml/2 tbsp lukewarm water
150ml/¼ pint/⅔ cup sour cream
1 egg, lightly beaten
50g/2oz/¼ cup butter, softened

FOR THE GLAZE
1 egg yolk
15ml/1 tbsp water

MAKES 1 LOAF

COOK'S TIP
If you prefer, use a 7g/¼ oz sachet of easy-blend (rapid-rise) dried yeast. Add directly to the flour with the salt, then add the warmed sour cream and water and mix together.

This braided, attractively tapered loaf is known as zupfe *in Switzerland.*
Often eaten at the weekend, it has a glossy crust and a wonderfully light crumb.

1 Lightly grease a baking sheet. Sift the flour and salt together into a large bowl and make a well in the centre. Mix the yeast with the water in a jug (pitcher).

2 Gently warm the sour cream in a small pan until it reaches blood heat (35–38°C). Add to the yeast mixture and mix together.

3 Add the yeast mixture and egg to the centre of the flour and gradually mix to a dough. Beat in the softened butter.

4 Turn out on to a lightly floured surface and knead for 5 minutes until smooth and elastic. Place in a lightly oiled bowl, cover with oiled clear film (plastic wrap) and leave in a warm place, for about 1½ hours, or until doubled in size.

5 Turn out on to a lightly floured surface and knock back (punch down). Cut in half and shape each piece of dough into a long rope about 35cm/14in in length.

6 To make the braid, place the two pieces of dough on top of each other to form a cross. Starting with the bottom rope, fold the top end over and place between the two bottom ropes. Fold the remaining top rope over so that all four ropes are pointing downwards. Starting from the left, braid the first rope over the second, and the third rope over the fourth.

7 Continue braiding in this way to form a tapered bread. Tuck the ends underneath and place on the prepared baking sheet. Cover with lightly oiled clear film and leave to rise, in a warm place, for about 40 minutes.

8 Meanwhile, preheat the oven to 190°C/375°F/Gas 5. Mix the egg yolk and water for the glaze, and brush over the loaf. Bake the bread for 30–35 minutes, or until golden. Cool on a wire rack.

PUMPERNICKEL

This famous German bread is extremely dense and dark, with an intense flavour. It is baked very slowly and although cooked in the oven, it is more like a steamed bread than a baked one.

450g/1lb/4 cups rye flour
225g/8oz/2 cups wholemeal
(whole-wheat) flour
115g/4oz/⅔ cup bulgur wheat
10ml/2 tsp salt
30ml/2 tbsp molasses
850ml/1 pint 8fl oz/3½ cups warm water
15ml/1 tbsp vegetable oil

MAKES 2 LOAVES

COOK'S TIP
This bread improves on keeping. Keep for at least 24 hours double-wrapped inside a plastic bag or greaseproof (waxed) paper and foil before slicing.

1 Lightly grease two 18 × 9cm/7 × 3½in loaf tins (pans). Mix the rye flour, wholemeal flour, bulgur wheat and salt together in a large bowl.

2 Mix the molasses with the warm water and add to the flours with the vegetable oil. Mix together to form a dense mass.

3 Place in the prepared tins, pressing well into the corners. Cover with lightly oiled clear film (plastic wrap) and leave in a warm place for 18–24 hours.

4 Preheat the oven to 110°C/225°F/ Gas ¼. Cover the tins tightly with foil. Fill a roasting pan with boiling water and place a rack on top.

5 Place the tins on top of the rack and transfer very carefully to the oven. Bake the loaves for 4 hours. Increase the oven temperature to 160°C/325°F/Gas 3. Top up the water in the roasting pan if necessary, uncover the loaves and bake for a further 30–45 minutes, or until the loaves feel firm and the tops are crusty.

6 Leave to cool in the tins for 5 minutes, then turn out on to a wire rack to cool completely. Serve cold, very thinly sliced, with cold meats.

GERMAN SOURDOUGH BREAD

This bread includes rye, wholemeal and plain flours for a superb depth of flavour. Serve it cut in thick slices, with creamy butter or a sharp cheese.

FOR THE SOURDOUGH STARTER
75g/3oz/3/4 cup rye flour
80ml/3fl oz/1/3 cup warm water
pinch caraway seeds

FOR THE DOUGH
15g/1/2 oz fresh yeast
315ml/11fl oz/11/3 cups lukewarm water
275g/10oz/21/2 cups rye flour
150g/5oz/11/4 cups wholemeal (whole-wheat) bread flour
150g/5oz/11/4 cups unbleached white bread flour
10ml/2 tsp salt

MAKES 1 LOAF

1 Mix the rye flour, warm water and caraway for the starter together in a large bowl with your fingertips, to make a soft paste. Cover with a damp dishtowel and leave in a warm place for about 36 hours. Stir after 24 hours.

2 Lightly grease a baking sheet. In a measuring jug (cup), blend the yeast for the dough with the lukewarm water. Add to the starter and mix thoroughly.

3 Mix the rye flour, wholemeal bread flour and unbleached white bread flour for the dough with the salt in a large bowl; make a well in the centre. Pour in the yeast liquid and gradually incorporate the surrounding flour to make a smooth dough.

4 Turn out the dough on to a lightly floured surface and knead for 8–10 minutes until smooth and elastic. Place in a lightly oiled bowl, cover with lightly oiled clear film (plastic wrap) and leave to rise, in a warm place, for 1½ hours, or until nearly doubled in bulk.

5 Turn out on to a lightly floured surface, knock back (punch down) and knead gently. Shape into a round and place in a floured basket or *couronne*, with the seam up. Cover with lightly oiled clear film and leave to rise, in a warm place, for 2–3 hours.

6 Meanwhile, preheat the oven to 200°C/400°F/Gas 6. Turn out the loaf on to the prepared baking sheet and bake for 35–40 minutes. Cool on a wire rack.

COOK'S TIP
Proving the dough in a floured basket or *couronne* gives it its characteristic patterned crust, but is not essential. Make sure that you flour the basket well, otherwise the dough may stick.

STOLLEN

This German speciality bread, made for the Christmas season, is rich with rum-soaked fruits and is wrapped around a moist almond filling. The folded shape of the dough over the filling represents the baby Jesus wrapped in swaddling clothes.

75g/3oz/1/2 cup sultanas (golden raisins)
50g/2oz/1/4 cup currants
45ml/3 tbsp rum
375g/13oz/31/4 cups unbleached white bread flour
2.5ml/1/2 tsp salt
50g/2oz/1/4 cup caster (superfine) sugar
1.5ml/1/4 tsp ground cardamom
2.5ml/1/2 tsp ground cinnamon
40g/11/2 oz fresh yeast
120ml/4fl oz/1/2 cup lukewarm milk
50g/2oz/1/4 cup butter, melted
1 egg, lightly beaten
50g/2oz/1/3 cup mixed (candied) peel
50g/2oz/1/3 cup blanched whole almonds, chopped
melted butter, for brushing
icing (confectioners') sugar to dust

FOR THE ALMOND FILLING
115g/4oz/1 cup ground almonds
50g/2oz/1/4 cup caster sugar
50g/2oz/1/2 cup icing sugar
2.5ml/1/2 tsp lemon juice
1/2 egg, lightly beaten

MAKES 1 LARGE LOAF

COOK'S TIP
You can dust the cooled stollen with icing sugar and cinnamon, or drizzle over a thin glacé icing.

1 Lightly grease a baking sheet. Preheat the oven to 180°C/350°F/Gas 4. Put the sultanas and currants in a heatproof bowl and warm for 3–4 minutes. Pour over the rum and set aside.

2 Sift the flour and salt together into a large bowl. Stir in the sugar and spices.

3 Mix the yeast with the milk until creamy. Pour into the flour and mix a little of the flour from around the edge into the milk mixture to make a thick batter. Sprinkle some of the remaining flour over the top of the batter, then cover with clear film (plastic wrap) and leave in a warm place for 30 minutes.

4 Add the melted butter and egg and mix to a soft dough. Turn out the dough on to a lightly floured surface and knead for 8–10 minutes until smooth and elastic. Place in a lightly oiled bowl, cover with lightly oiled clear film and leave to rise, in a warm place, for 2–3 hours, or until doubled in bulk.

5 Mix the ground almonds and sugars together for the filling. Add the lemon juice and sufficient egg to knead to a smooth paste. Shape into a 20cm/8in long sausage, cover and set aside.

6 Turn out the dough on to a lightly floured surface and knock back (punch down).

7 Pat out the dough into a rectangle about 2.5cm/1in thick and sprinkle over the sultanas, currants, mixed peel and almonds. Fold and knead the dough to incorporate the fruit and nuts.

8 Roll out the dough into an oval about 30 × 23cm/12 × 9in. Roll the centre slightly thinner than the edges. Place the almond paste filling along the centre and fold over the dough to enclose it, making sure that the top of the dough doesn't completely cover the base. The top edge should be slightly in from the bottom edge. Press down to seal.

9 Place the loaf on the prepared baking sheet, cover with lightly oiled clear film and leave to rise, in a warm place, for 45–60 minutes, or until doubled in size.

10 Meanwhile, preheat the oven to 200°C/400°F/Gas 6. Bake the loaf for about 30 minutes, or until it sounds hollow when tapped on the base. Brush the top with melted butter and transfer to a wire rack to cool. Dust with icing sugar just before serving.

PRETZELS

---

*Pretzels or brezeln, as they are known in Germany, are said to be derived
from the Latin bracellae or arms, referring to the crossed "arms" of dough
inside the oval shape. This shape is also used for biscuits in Germany and
Austria, and in Alsace the pretzel shape is part of the wrought iron emblem of
quality that bakers display outside their shops.*

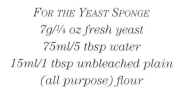

FOR THE YEAST SPONGE
7g/¼ oz fresh yeast
75ml/5 tbsp water
15ml/1 tbsp unbleached plain
(all purpose) flour

FOR THE DOUGH
7g/¼ oz fresh yeast
150ml/¼ pint/⅔ cup lukewarm water
75ml/5 tbsp lukewarm milk
400g/14oz/3½ cups unbleached white
bread flour
7.5ml/1½ tsp salt
25g/1oz/2 tbsp butter, melted

FOR THE TOPPING
1 egg yolk
15ml/1 tbsp milk
sea salt or caraway seeds

MAKES 12 PRETZELS

1 Lightly flour a baking sheet. Also
grease two baking sheets. Cream the
yeast for the yeast sponge with the
water, then mix in the flour, cover with
clear film (plastic wrap) and leave to
stand at room temperature for 2 hours.

2 Mix the yeast for the dough with the
water until dissolved, then stir in the
milk. Sift 350g/12oz/3 cups of the flour
and the salt into a large bowl. Add the
yeast sponge mixture and the butter;
mix for 3–4 minutes. Turn out on to a
lightly floured surface and knead in the
remaining flour to make a medium firm
dough. Place in a lightly oiled bowl, cover
with lightly oiled clear film and leave to
rise, in a warm place, for 30 minutes, or
until almost doubled in bulk.

3 Turn out on to a lightly floured surface
and knock back (punch down) the dough.
Knead into a ball, return to the bowl,
re-cover and leave to rise for 30 minutes.

4 Turn out the dough on to a lightly
floured surface. Divide the dough into
12 equal pieces and form into balls.
Take one ball of dough and cover the
remainder with a dishtowel. Roll into a
thin stick 46cm/18in long and about
1cm/½ in thick in the middle and thinner
at the ends. Bend each end of the dough
stick into a horseshoe. Cross over and
place the ends on top of the thick part of
the pretzel. Repeat with the remaining
dough balls.

5 Place on the floured baking sheet to
rest for 10 minutes. Meanwhile, preheat
the oven to 190°C/375°F/Gas 5. Bring a
large pan of water to the boil, then
reduce to a simmer. Add the pretzels to
the simmering water in batches, about
2–3 at a time and poach for about
1 minute. Drain the pretzels on a
dishtowel and place on the greased
baking sheets, spaced well apart.

6 Mix the egg yolk and milk together
and brush this glaze over the pretzels.
Sprinkle with sea salt or caraway seeds
and bake the pretzels for 25 minutes, or
until they are deep golden. Transfer to a
wire rack to cool.

BUCHTY

*450g/1lb/4 cups unbleached white
bread flour
5ml/1 tsp salt
50g/2oz/¼ cup caster (superfine) sugar
90g/3½oz/scant ½ cup butter
120ml/4fl oz/½ cup milk
20g/¾ oz fresh yeast
3 eggs, lightly beaten
40g/1½ oz/3 tbsp butter, melted
icing (confectioners') sugar, for dusting*

MAKES 16 ROLLS

COOK'S TIP
If you do not have a square tin use a
round one. Place two rolls in the
centre and the rest around the edge.

*Popular in both Poland and Germany as breakfast treats, these are also
excellent split and toasted, and served with cured meats.*

1 Grease a 20cm/8in square loose-bottomed cake tin (pan). Sift the flour and salt together into a large bowl and stir in the sugar. Make a well in the centre.

2 Melt 50g/2oz/¼ cup of the butter in a small pan, then remove from the heat and stir in the milk. Leave to cool until lukewarm. Stir the yeast into the milk mixture until it has dissolved.

3 Pour into the centre of the flour and stir in sufficient flour to form a thick batter. Sprinkle with a little of the surrounding flour, cover and leave in a warm place for 30 minutes.

4 Gradually beat in the eggs and remaining flour to form a soft, smooth dough. This will take about 10 minutes. Cover with oiled clear film (plastic wrap) and leave in a warm place, for about 1½ hours, or until doubled in bulk.

5 Turn out the dough on to a lightly floured surface and knock back (punch down). Divide into 16 equal pieces and shape into rounds. Melt the remaining butter, roll the rounds in it to coat, then place, slightly apart, in the tin. Cover with lightly oiled clear film and leave to rise, in a warm place, for about 1 hour, or until doubled.

6 Meanwhile, preheat the oven to 190°C/375°F/Gas 5. Spoon any remaining melted butter evenly over the rolls and bake for 25 minutes, or until golden brown. Turn out on to a wire rack to cool. If serving buchty as a breakfast bread, dust the loaf with icing sugar before separating it into rolls.

POLISH RYE BREAD

This rye bread is made with half white flour which gives it a lighter, more open texture than a traditional rye loaf. Served thinly sliced, it is the perfect accompaniment for cold meats and fish.

225g/8oz/2 cups rye flour
225g/8oz/2 cups unbleached white bread flour
10ml/2 tsp caraway seeds
10ml/2 tsp salt
20g/¾ oz fresh yeast
140ml/scant ¼ pint/scant ⅔ cup lukewarm milk
5ml/1 tsp clear honey
140ml/scant ¼ pint/scant ⅔ cup lukewarm water
wholemeal (whole-wheat) flour, to dust

MAKES 1 LOAF

4 Turn out the dough on to a lightly floured surface and knock back (punch down). Shape into an oval loaf and place on the prepared baking sheet.

5 Dust with wholemeal flour, cover with lightly oiled clear film and leave to rise, in a warm place, for 1–1½ hours, or until doubled in size. Meanwhile, preheat the oven to 220°C/425°F/Gas 7.

1 Lightly grease a baking sheet. Mix the flours, caraway seeds and salt in a large bowl and make a well in the centre.

2 In a bowl or measuring jug (cup), cream the yeast with the milk and honey. Pour into the centre of the flour, add the water and gradually incorporate the surrounding flour and caraway mixture until a dough forms.

3 Turn out the dough on to a lightly floured surface and knead for 8–10 minutes until smooth, elastic and firm. Place in a large, lightly oiled bowl, cover with lightly oiled clear film (plastic wrap) and leave in a warm place, for about 3 hours, or until doubled in bulk.

6 Using a sharp knife, slash the loaf with two long cuts about 2.5cm/1in apart. Bake for 30–35 minutes, or until the loaf sounds hollow when tapped on the base. Transfer the loaf to a wire rack and set aside to cool.

RUSSIAN POTATO BREAD

In Russia, potatoes are often used to replace some of the flour in bread recipes. They endow the bread with excellent keeping qualities.

1 Lightly grease a baking sheet. Add the potatoes to a pan of boiling water and cook until tender. Drain and reserve 150ml/¼ pint/⅔ cup of the cooking water. Mash and sieve the potatoes and leave to cool.

2 Mix the yeast, bread flours, caraway seeds and salt together in a large bowl. Add the butter and rub in. Mix the reserved potato water and sieved potatoes together. Gradually work this mixture into the flour mixture to form a soft dough.

3 Turn out on to a lightly floured surface and knead for 8–10 minutes until smooth and elastic. Place in a lightly oiled bowl, cover with oiled clear film (plastic wrap) and leave in a warm place, for 1 hour, or until doubled in bulk.

4 Turn out on to a lightly floured surface, knock back (punch down) and knead gently. Shape into a plump oval loaf, about 18cm/7in long. Place on the prepared baking sheet and sprinkle with a little wholemeal bread flour.

5 Cover the dough with lightly oiled clear film and leave to rise, in a warm place, for 30 minutes, or until doubled in size. Meanwhile, preheat the oven to 200°C/400°F/Gas 6.

6 Using a sharp knife, slash the top with 3–4 diagonal cuts to make a criss-cross effect. Bake for 30–35 minutes, or until golden and sounding hollow when tapped on the base. Transfer to a wire rack to cool.

225g/8oz potatoes, peeled and diced
7g/¼ oz sachet easy-blend (rapid-rise) dried yeast
350g/12oz/3 cups unbleached white bread flour
115g/4oz/1 cup wholemeal (whole-wheat) bread flour, plus extra for sprinkling
2.5ml/½ tsp caraway seeds, crushed
10ml/2 tsp salt
25g/1oz/2 tbsp butter

MAKES 1 LOAF

VARIATION
To make a cheese-flavoured potato bread, omit the caraway seeds and knead 115g/4oz/1 cup grated Cheddar, Red Leicester or a crumbled blue cheese, such as Stilton, into the dough before shaping.

SUNSHINE LOAF

Scandinavia, Land of the Midnight Sun, has numerous breads based on rye. This splendid table centrepiece is made with a blend of rye and white flours, the latter helping to lighten the bread.

FOR THE STARTER
60ml/4 tbsp lukewarm milk
60ml/4 tbsp lukewarm water
7g/¹/₄ oz fresh yeast
100g/3¾oz/scant 1 cup unbleached white bread flour

FOR THE DOUGH
15g/¹/₂ oz fresh yeast
500ml/17fl oz/generous 2 cups lukewarm water
450g/1lb/4 cups rye flour
225g/8oz/2 cups unbleached white bread flour
15ml/1 tbsp salt
milk, for glazing
caraway seeds, for sprinkling

MAKES 1 LARGE LOAF

VARIATION
This bread can be shaped into one large round or oval loaf, if preferred.

1 Combine the milk and water for the starter in a large bowl. Mix in the yeast until dissolved. Gradually add the bread flour, stirring it with a metal spoon.

2 Cover the bowl with clear film (plastic wrap) and leave the mixture in a warm place for 3–4 hours, or until well risen, bubbly and starting to collapse.

3 Mix the yeast for the dough with 60ml/4 tbsp of the water until creamy, then stir in the remaining water. Gradually mix into the starter to dilute it. Gradually mix in the rye flour to form a smooth batter. Cover with lightly oiled clear film and leave in a warm place, for 3–4 hours, or until well risen.

4 Stir the bread flour and salt into the batter to form a dough. Turn on to a lightly floured surface and knead for 5 minutes until smooth and elastic. Place in a lightly oiled bowl, cover with lightly oiled clear film and leave to rise, in a warm place, for about 1 hour, or until doubled in bulk.

5 Knock back (punch down) on a lightly floured surface. Cut the dough into five pieces. Roll one piece into a 50cm/20in "sausage" and roll up into a spiral shape.

6 Cut the remaining pieces of dough in half and shape each one into a 20cm/8in rope. Place in a circle on a large baking sheet, spaced equally apart, like rays of the sun, and curl the ends round, leaving a small gap in the centre. Place the spiral shape on top. Cover with lightly oiled clear film and leave to rise, in a warm place, for 30 minutes.

7 Meanwhile, preheat the oven to 230°C/450°F/Gas 8. Brush the bread with milk, sprinkle with caraway seeds and bake for 30 minutes, or until lightly browned. Transfer to a wire rack to cool.

SAVOURY DANISH CROWN

Filled with golden onions and cheese, this butter-rich bread ring is quite irresistible and needs no accompaniment.

1 Lightly grease a baking sheet. Sift the flour and salt together into a large bowl. Rub in 40g/1½ oz/3 tbsp of the butter. Mix the yeast with the milk and water. Add to the flour with the egg and mix to a soft dough.

2 Turn out on to a lightly floured surface and knead for 10 minutes until smooth and elastic. Place in a lightly oiled bowl, cover with lightly oiled clear film (plastic wrap) and leave to rise, in a warm place, for about 1 hour, or until doubled in bulk.

3 Knock back (punch down) and turn out on to a lightly floured surface. Roll out into an oblong about 1cm/½ in thick.

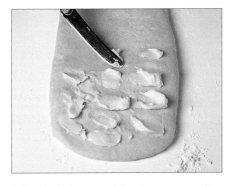

4 Dot half the remaining butter over the top two-thirds of the dough. Fold the bottom third up and the top third down and seal the edges. Turn by 90 degrees and repeat with the remaining butter. Fold and seal as before. Cover the dough with lightly oiled clear film and leave to rest for about 15 minutes.

5 Turn by a further 90 degrees. Roll and fold again without any butter. Repeat once more. Wrap in lightly oiled clear film and leave to rest in the refrigerator for 30 minutes.

6 Meanwhile, heat the oil for the filling. Add the onions and cook for 10 minutes until soft and golden. Remove from the heat and stir in the breadcrumbs, almonds, Parmesan and seasoning.

7 Add half the beaten egg to the breadcrumb mixture and bind together.

8 Roll out the dough on a lightly floured surface into a rectangle measuring 56 × 23cm/22 × 9in. Spread with the filling to within 2cm/¾ in of the edges, then roll up like a Swiss (jelly) roll from one long side. Using a very sharp knife, cut in half lengthways. Braid together with the cut sides up and shape into a ring. Place on the prepared baking sheet, cover with lightly oiled clear film and leave to rise, in a warm place, for 30 minutes.

9 Meanwhile, preheat the oven to 200°C/400°F/Gas 6. Brush the remaining beaten egg over the dough. Sprinkle with sesame seeds and Parmesan cheese and bake for 40–50 minutes, or until golden. Transfer to a wire rack to cool slightly if serving warm, or cool completely to serve cold, cut into slices.

350g/12oz/3 cups unbleached white bread flour
5ml/1 tsp salt
185g/6½ oz/generous ¾ cup butter, softened
20g/¾ oz fresh yeast
200ml/7fl oz/scant 1 cup mixed lukewarm milk and water
1 egg, lightly beaten

FOR THE FILLING
30ml/2 tbsp sunflower oil
2 onions, finely chopped
40g/1½ oz/¾ cup fresh breadcrumbs
25g/1oz/¼ cup ground almonds
50g/2oz/½ cup freshly grated Parmesan cheese
1 egg, lightly beaten
salt and freshly ground black pepper

FOR THE TOPPING
15ml/1 tbsp sesame seeds
15ml/1 tbsp freshly grated Parmesan cheese

MAKES 1 LARGE LOAF

BAGELS

Bagels are eaten in many countries, especially where there is a Jewish community, and are very popular in the USA. They can be made from white, wholemeal or rye flour and finished with a variety of toppings, including caraway, poppy seeds, sesame seeds and onion.

350g/12oz/3 cups unbleached white bread flour
10ml/2 tsp salt
6g/1/4 oz sachet easy-blend (rapid-rise) dried yeast
5ml/1 tsp malt extract
210ml/71/2 fl oz/scant 1 cup lukewarm water

FOR POACHING
2.5 litres/4 pints/21/2 quarts water
15ml/1 tbsp malt extract

FOR THE TOPPING
1 egg white
10ml/2 tsp cold water
30ml/2 tbsp poppy, sesame or caraway seeds

MAKES 10 BAGELS

5 Meanwhile, preheat the oven to 220°C/425°F/Gas 7. Place the water and malt extract for poaching in a large pan, bring to the boil, then reduce to a simmer. Place the bagels in the water two or three at a time and poach for about 1 minute. They will sink and then rise again when first added to the pan. Using a spatula or large slotted spoon, turn over and cook for 30 seconds. Remove and drain on a dishtowel. Repeat with the rest.

1 Grease two baking sheets. Sift the flour and salt together into a large bowl. Stir in the dried yeast. Make a well in the centre. Mix the malt extract and water, add to the centre of the flour and mix to a dough. Knead on a floured surface until elastic.

2 Place in a lightly oiled bowl, cover with lightly oiled clear film (plastic wrap) and leave in a warm place, for about 1 hour, or until doubled in bulk.

3 Turn out on to a lightly floured surface and knock back (punch down). Knead for 1 minute, then divide into 10 equal pieces. Shape into balls, cover with clear film and leave to rest for 5 minutes.

4 Gently flatten each ball and make a hole through the centre with your thumb. Enlarge the hole slightly by turning your thumb around. Place on a floured tray; re-cover and leave in a warm place, for 10–20 minutes, or until they begin to rise.

6 Place five bagels on each prepared baking sheet, spacing them well apart. Beat the egg white with the water for the topping, brush the mixture over the top of each bagel and sprinkle with poppy, sesame or caraway seeds. Bake for 20–25 minutes, or until golden brown. Transfer the bagels to a wire rack to cool.

CHALLAH

Challah is an egg-rich, light-textured bread baked for the Jewish Sabbath and to celebrate religious holidays. It is usually braided with three or four strands of dough, but eight strands or more may be used to create especially festive loaves.

500g/1¼ lb/5 cups unbleached white bread flour
10ml/2 tsp salt
20g/¾ oz fresh yeast
200ml/7fl oz/scant 1 cup lukewarm water
30ml/2 tbsp caster (superfine) sugar
2 eggs
75g/3oz/6 tbsp butter or margarine, melted

FOR THE GLAZE
1 egg yolk
15ml/1 tbsp water
10ml/2 tsp poppy seeds, for sprinkling

MAKES 1 LARGE LOAF

COOK'S TIP
If wished, divide the dough in half and make two small challah, keeping the braids quite simple. Decorate with the poppy seeds or leave plain. Reduce the baking time by about 10 minutes.

1 Lightly grease a baking sheet. Sift the flour and salt together into a large bowl and make a well in the centre. Mix the yeast with the water and sugar, add to the centre of the flour with the eggs and melted butter or margarine and gradually mix in the surrounding flour to form a soft dough.

2 Turn out on to a lightly floured surface and knead for 10 minutes until smooth and elastic. Place in a lightly oiled bowl, cover with lightly oiled clear film (plastic wrap) and leave in a warm place, for 1 hour, or until doubled in bulk.

3 Knock back (punch down), re-cover and leave to rise again in a warm place for about 1 hour. Knock back, turn out on to a lightly floured surface and knead gently. Divide into four equal pieces. Roll each piece into a rope about 45cm/18in long. Line up next to each other. Pinch the ends together at one end.

4 Starting from the right, lift the first rope over the second and the third rope over the fourth. Take the fourth rope and place it between the first and second ropes. Repeat, starting from the right, and continue until braided.

5 Tuck the ends under and place the loaf on the prepared baking sheet. Cover with lightly oiled clear film and leave to rise in a warm place, for about 30–45 minutes, or until doubled in size. Meanwhile, preheat the oven to 200°C/400°F/Gas 6. Beat the egg yolk and water for the glaze together.

6 Brush the egg glaze gently over the loaf. Sprinkle evenly with the poppy seeds and bake for 35–40 minutes, or until the challah is a deep golden brown. Transfer to a wire rack and leave to cool before slicing.

SAN FRANCISCO SOURDOUGH BREAD

In San Francisco this bread is leavened using a flour and water paste, which is left to ferment with the aid of airborne yeast. The finished loaves have a moist crumb and crispy crust, and will keep for several days.

FOR THE STARTER
50g/2oz/¹/₂ cup wholemeal (whole-wheat) flour
pinch of ground cumin
15ml/1 tbsp milk
15–30ml/1–2 tbsp water
1ST REFRESHMENT
30ml/2 tbsp water
115g/4oz/1 cup wholemeal flour
2ND REFRESHMENT
60ml/4 tbsp water
115g/4oz/1 cup white bread flour

FOR THE BREAD: 1ST REFRESHMENT
75ml/5 tbsp very warm water
75g/3oz/³/₄ cup unbleached plain (all-purpose) flour
2ND REFRESHMENT
175ml/6fl oz/³/₄ cup lukewarm water
200–225g/7–8oz/1³/₄–2 cups unbleached plain flour

FOR THE SOURDOUGH
280ml/9fl oz/1¹/₄ cups warm water
500g/1¹/₄lb/5 cups unbleached white bread flour
15ml/1 tbsp salt
flour, for dusting
ice cubes, for baking

MAKES 2 ROUND LOAVES

1 Sift the flour and cumin for the starter into a bowl. Add the milk and sufficient water to make a firm but moist dough. Knead for 6–8 minutes to form a firm dough. Return the dough to the bowl, cover with a damp dishtowel and leave in a warm place, 24–26°C/75–80°F, for about 2 days. When it is ready the starter will appear moist and wrinkled and will have developed a crust.

2 Pull off the hardened crust and discard. Scoop out the moist centre (about the size of a hazelnut), which will be aerated and sweet smelling, and place in a clean bowl. Mix in the water for the 1st refreshment. Gradually add the wholemeal flour and mix to a dough.

3 Cover with clear film (plastic wrap) and return to a warm place for 1–2 days. Discard the crust and gradually mix in the water for the 2nd refreshment to the starter, which by now will have a slightly sharper smell. Gradually mix in the white flour, cover and leave in a warm place for 8–10 hours.

4 For the bread, mix the sourdough starter with the water for the 1st refreshment. Gradually mix in the flour to form a firm dough. Knead for 6–8 minutes until firm. Cover with a damp dishtowel and leave in a warm place for 8–12 hours, or until doubled in bulk.

5 Gradually mix in the water for the 2nd refreshment, then gradually mix in enough flour to form a soft, smooth elastic dough. Re-cover and leave in a warm place for 8–12 hours. Gradually stir in the water for the sourdough, then gradually work in the flour and salt. This will take 10–15 minutes. Turn out on to a lightly floured surface and knead until smooth and very elastic. Place in a large lightly oiled bowl, cover with lightly oiled clear film and leave to rise, in a warm place, for 8–12 hours.

6 Divide the dough in half and shape into two round loaves by folding the sides over to the centre and sealing.

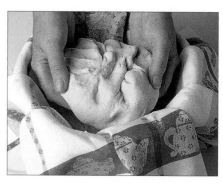

7 Place seam side up in flour-dusted *couronnes*, bowls or baskets lined with flour-dusted dish towels. Re-cover and leave to rise in a warm place for 4 hours.

8 Preheat the oven to 220°C/425°F/Gas 7. Place an empty roasting pan in the bottom of the oven. Dust two baking sheets with flour. Turn out the loaves seam side down on the prepared baking sheets. Using a sharp knife, cut a criss-cross pattern by slashing the top of the loaves four or five times in each direction.

9 Place the baking sheets in the oven and immediately drop the ice cubes into the hot roasting pan to create steam. Bake the bread for 25 minutes, then reduce the oven temperature to 200°C/400°F/Gas 6 and bake for a further 15–20 minutes, or until sounding hollow when tapped on the base. Transfer to wire racks to cool.

COOK'S TIP
If you'd like to make sourdough bread regularly, keep a small amount of the starter covered in the refrigerator. It will keep for several days. Use the starter for the 2nd refreshment, then continue as directed.

ANADAMA BREAD

A traditional bread from Massachusetts, made with molasses, cornmeal, wholemeal and unbleached white flour. According to legend, it was created by the husband of a woman called Anna, who had left a corn meal mush and some molasses in the kitchen. On finding only these ingredients for supper her husband mixed them with some flour, water and yeast to make this bread, while muttering "Anna, damn her"!

40g/1½ oz/3 tbsp butter
120ml/4fl oz/½ cup molasses
560ml/scant 1 pint/scant 2½ cups water
50g/2oz/½ cup cornmeal
10ml/2 tsp salt
25g/1oz fresh yeast
30ml/2 tbsp lukewarm water
275g/10oz/2½ cups wholemeal (whole-wheat) flour
450g/1lb/4 cups unbleached white bread flour

MAKES 2 LOAVES

1 Grease two 1.5 litre/2½ pint/6 cup loaf tins (pans). Heat the butter, molasses and measured water in a pan until the butter has melted. Stir in the corn meal and salt and stir over a low heat until boiling. Cool until lukewarm.

2 In a small bowl, cream the yeast with the lukewarm water, then set aside for 5 minutes.

3 Mix the corn meal mixture and yeast mixture together in a large bowl. Fold in the wholemeal flour and then the unbleached white bread flour to form a sticky dough. Turn out on to a lightly floured surface and knead for 10–15 minutes until the dough is smooth and elastic. Add a little more flour if needed.

4 Place in a lightly oiled bowl, cover with lightly oiled clear film (plastic wrap) and leave in a warm place, for about 1 hour, or until doubled in bulk.

VARIATION
Use a 7g/¼ oz sachet easy-blend (rapid-rise) dried yeast instead of fresh. Mix it with the wholemeal flour. Add to the corn meal mixture, then add the lukewarm water, which would conventionally be blended with the fresh yeast.

5 Knead the dough lightly on a well floured surface, shape into two loaves and place in the prepared tins. Cover with lightly oiled clear film and leave to rise, in a warm place, for about 35–45 minutes, or until doubled in size and the dough reaches the top of the tins.

6 Meanwhile, preheat the oven to 200°C/400°F/Gas 6. Using a sharp knife, slash the tops of the loaves three or four times. Bake for 15 minutes, then reduce the oven temperature to 180°C/350°F/Gas 4 and bake for a further 35–40 minutes, or until sounding hollow when tapped on the base. Turn out on to a wire rack to cool slightly. Serve warm.

BOSTON BROWN BREAD

Rich, moist and dark, this bread is flavoured with molasses and can include raisins. In Boston it is often served with savoury baked beans.

90g/3½ oz/scant 1 cup corn meal
90g/3½ oz/scant 1 cup unbleached plain (all-purpose) white flour or wholemeal (whole-wheat) flour
90g/3½ oz/scant 1 cup rye flour
2.5ml/½ tsp salt
5ml/1 tsp bicarbonate of soda (baking soda)
90g/3½ oz/generous ½ cup raisins
120ml/4fl oz/½ cup milk
120ml/4fl oz/½ cup water
120ml/4fl oz/½ cup molasses

MAKES 1 OR 2 LOAVES

COOK'S TIP
If you do not have empty coffee jugs, cans or similar moulds, cook the bread in one or two heatproof bowls of equivalent capacity.

1 Line the base of one 1.2 litre/2 pint/ 5 cup cylindrical metal or glass container, such as a heatproof glass coffee jug (carafe), with greased greaseproof (waxed) paper. Alternatively, remove the lids from two 450g/1lb coffee cans, wash and dry them thoroughly, then line with greased greaseproof paper.

2 Mix together the corn meal, plain or wholemeal flour, rye flour, salt, bicarbonate of soda and raisins in a large bowl. Warm the milk and water in a small pan and stir in the molasses.

3 Add the molasses mixture to the dry ingredients and mix together using a spoon until it just forms a moist dough. Do not overmix.

4 Fill the jug or cans with the dough; they should be about two-thirds full. Cover neatly with foil or greased greaseproof paper and tie securely.

5 Bring water to a depth of 5cm/2in to the boil in a deep, heavy pan large enough to accommodate the jug or cans.

6 Place a trivet in the pan, stand the jug or cans on top, cover the pan and steam for 1½ hours, adding more boiling water to maintain the required level as necessary.

7 Cool the loaves for a few minutes in the jug or cans, then turn them on their sides and the loaves should slip out. Serve warm, as a teabread or with savoury dishes.

*225g/8oz/2 cups unbleached plain
(all-purpose) flour
5ml/1 tsp salt
4ml/³/₄ tsp baking powder
40g/1¹/₂ oz/3 tbsp lard (shortening)
or vegetable fat
150ml/¹/₄ pint/²/₃ cup warm water*

MAKES 12 TORTILLAS

COOK'S TIPS
• Tortillas are delicious either as an accompaniment or filled with roast chicken or cooked minced (ground) meat, refried beans and/or salad to serve as a snack or light lunch.
• To reheat tortillas, wrap in foil and warm in a moderate oven, 180°C/350°F/Gas 4, for about 5 minutes.

WHEAT TORTILLAS

Tortillas are the staple flat bread in Mexico, where they are often made from masa harina, a flour milled from corn. These soft wheat tortillas are also popular in the South-western states of the USA.

1 Mix the flour, salt and baking powder in a bowl. Rub in the fat, stir in the water and knead lightly to a soft dough. Cover with clear film (plastic wrap) and leave to rest for 15 minutes. Divide into 12 pieces and shape into balls. Roll out on a floured surface into 15–18cm/ 6–7in rounds. Re-cover to keep moist.

2 Heat a heavy frying pan or griddle, add one tortilla and cook for 1¹/₂–2 minutes, turning over as soon as the surface starts to bubble. It should stay flexible. Remove from the pan and wrap in a dishtowel to keep warm while cooking the remaining tortillas in the same way.

---

*75g/3oz/³/₄ cup unbleached white
bread flour
150g/6oz/1¹/₂ cups yellow cornmeal
5ml/1 tsp salt
25ml/1¹/₂ tbsp baking powder
15ml/1 tbsp caster (superfine) sugar
50g/2oz/4 tbsp butter, melted
250ml/8fl oz/1 cup milk
3 eggs
200g/7oz/scant 1¹/₄ cups canned corn,
drained*

MAKES 1 LARGE LOAF

VARIATIONS
• Bake this corn bread in a 20cm/8in square cake tin (pan) instead of a round one if you wish to cut it into squares or rectangles.
• If you would prefer a more rustic corn bread, replace some or all of the white bread flour with wholemeal (whole-wheat) bread flour.

DOUBLE CORN BREAD

In the American South, corn bread is made with white corn meal and is fairly flat, while in the North it is thicker and made with yellow cornmeal. Whatever the version it's delicious – this recipe combines yellow cornmeal with sweetcorn. It is marvellous served warm, cut into wedges and buttered.

1 Preheat the oven to 200°C/400°F/ Gas 6. Grease and base line a 22cm/ 8¹/₂ in round cake tin (pan). Sift the flour, corn meal, salt and baking powder together into a large bowl. Stir in the sugar and make a well in the centre.

3 Using a wooden spoon, stir the canned corn quickly into the mixture. Pour into the prepared tin and bake for 20–25 minutes, or until a metal skewer inserted into the centre comes out clean.

2 Mix the melted butter, milk and eggs together. Add to the centre of the flour mixture and beat until just combined.

4 Invert the bread on to a wire rack and lift off the lining paper. Cool slightly. Serve warm, cut into wedges.

TANDOORI ROTIS

There are numerous varieties of breads in India, most of them unleavened. This one, as its name suggests, would normally be baked in a tandoor – a clay oven which is heated with charcoal or wood. The oven becomes extremely hot, cooking the bread in minutes.

350g/12oz/3 cups atta or fine wholemeal (whole-wheat) flour
5ml/1 tsp salt
250ml/8fl oz/1 cup water
30–45ml/2–3 tbsp melted ghee or butter, for brushing

MAKES 6 ROTIS

COOK'S TIP
The rotis are ready when light brown bubbles appear on the surface.

1 Sift the flour and salt into a bowl. Add the water and mix to a soft dough. Knead on a lightly floured surface for 3–4 minutes until smooth. Place in a lightly oiled bowl, cover with oiled clear film (plastic wrap); leave for 1 hour.

2 Turn out on to a lightly floured surface. Divide the dough into six pieces and shape each into a ball. Press out into a larger round with the palm of your hand, cover with lightly oiled clear film and leave to rest for 10 minutes.

3 Meanwhile, preheat the oven to 230°C/450°F/Gas 8. Place three baking sheets in the oven to heat. Roll the rotis into 15cm/6in rounds, place two on each sheet and bake for 8–10 minutes. Brush with ghee or butter and serve warm.

PARATHAS

These triangular-shaped breads, made from a similar dough to that used for chapatis, are enriched with layers of ghee or butter to create a wonderfully rich, flaky bread.

1 Sift the flours and salt together into a large bowl. Add the oil with sufficient water to mix to a soft dough. Turn out the dough on to a lightly floured surface and knead vigorously for 8–10 minutes until smooth.

2 Place in a lightly oiled bowl and cover with a damp dishtowel. Leave to rest for 30 minutes.

3 Turn out on to a lightly floured surface. Divide the dough into nine equal pieces. Cover eight pieces of dough with oiled clear film (plastic wrap). Shape the remaining piece into a ball and then flatten it. Roll into a 15cm/6in round.

4 Brush with a little of the melted ghee or clarified butter and fold in half. Brush and fold again to form a triangular shape. Repeat with the remaining dough. Stack, layered between clear film, to keep moist. Heat a griddle or heavy frying pan.

115g/4oz/1¼ cups unbleached plain (all-purpose) flour
115g/4oz/1 cup wholemeal (whole-wheat) flour
2.5ml/½ tsp salt
15ml/1 tbsp vegetable oil
120–150ml/4–5fl oz/½–⅔ cup water
90–120ml/3–4fl oz/scant ½ cup melted ghee or clarified butter

MAKES 9 PARATHAS

5 Keeping the shape, roll each piece of dough to a larger triangle, each side measuring 15–18cm/6–7in. Brush with ghee or butter and place on the griddle or in the pan, brushed side down. Cook for about 1 minute, brush again and turn over. Cook for about 1 minute, or until crisp and dotted with brown speckles. Keep warm in a low oven while cooking the remaining parathas. Serve warm.

*225g/8oz/2 cups unbleached white
bread flour
2.5ml/¹⁄₂ tsp salt
15g/¹⁄₂ oz fresh yeast
60ml/4 tbsp lukewarm milk
15ml/1 tbsp vegetable oil
30ml/2 tbsp natural (plain) yogurt
1 egg
30–45ml/2–3 tbsp melted ghee or
butter, for brushing*

MAKES 3 NAAN

VARIATIONS
You can flavour naan in numerous
different ways:
• To make spicy naan, add 5ml/1 tsp
each ground coriander and ground
cumin to the flour in step 1. If you
would like the naan to be extra
fiery, add 2.5–5ml/¹⁄₂–1 tsp hot
chilli powder.
• To make cardamom-flavoured naan,
lightly crush the seeds from
4–5 green cardamom pods and add
to the flour in step 1.
• To make poppy seed naan, brush
the rolled-out naan with a little ghee
and sprinkle with poppy seeds. Press
lightly to make sure that they stick.
• To make peppered naan, brush the
rolled-out naan with a little ghee and
dust generously with coarsely ground
black pepper.
• To make onion-flavoured naan, add
114g/4oz/¹⁄₂ cup finely chopped or
coarsely grated onion to the dough in
step 2. You may need to reduce the
amount of egg if the onion is very
moist to prevent making the
dough too soft.
• To make wholemeal naan, substitute
wholemeal (whole-wheat) bread flour
for some or all of the white flour.

NAAN

*From the Caucasus through the Punjab region of northwest India and
beyond, all serve these leavened breads. Traditionally cooked in a very hot
clay oven known as a tandoor, naan are usually eaten with dry meat or
vegetable dishes, such as tandoori.*

1 Sift the flour and salt together into a
large bowl. In a smaller bowl, cream the
yeast with the milk. Set aside for
15 minutes.

2 Add the yeast mixture, oil, yogurt and
egg to the flour and mix to a soft dough.

3 Turn out the dough on to a lightly
floured surface and knead for about
10 minutes until smooth and elastic.
Place in a lightly oiled bowl, cover with
lightly oiled clear film (plastic wrap) and
leave to rise, in a warm place, for 45
minutes, or until doubled in bulk.

4 Preheat the oven to its highest setting,
at least 230°C/450°F/Gas 8. Place three
heavy baking sheets in the oven to heat.

5 Turn the dough out on to a lightly floured
surface and knock back (punch down).
Divide into three and shape into balls.

6 Cover two of the balls of dough with
oiled clear film and roll out the third into
a teardrop shape about 25cm/10in long,
13cm/5in wide and with a thickness of
about 5mm–8mm/¹⁄₄–¹⁄₃in.

7 Preheat the grill (broiler) to its
highest setting. Meanwhile, place the
naan on the hot baking sheets and bake
for 3–4 minutes, or until puffed up.

8 Remove the naan from the oven
and place under the hot grill for a few
seconds, or until the top of the naan
browns slightly. Wrap the cooked naan
in a dishtowel to keep warm while
rolling out and cooking the remaining
naan. Brush with melted ghee or butter
and serve warm.

COOK'S TIP
To help the naan dough to puff up
and brown, place the baking sheets in
an oven preheated to the maximum
temperature for at least 10 minutes
before baking to ensure that they are
hot. Preheat the grill while the naan
are baking.

INDEX